MY
BLACK BRITISH EXPERIENCE

Aired and Shared

by
Richard Anthony Todd

Edited By
Valerie Todd

Printed in Victoria, BC, Canada

Note for Librarians: a cataloguing record for this book that includes Dewey Decimal Classification and US Library of Congress numbers is available from the Library and Archives of Canada. The complete cataloguing record can be obtained from their online database at:
www.collectionscanada.ca/amicus/index-e.html
ISBN 1-4120-2958-9

TRAFFORD

This book was published *on-demand* in cooperation with Trafford Publishing. On-demand publishing is a unique process and service of making a book available for retail sale to the public taking advantage of on-demand manufacturing and Internet marketing. On-demand publishing includes promotions, retail sales, manufacturing, order fulfilment, accounting and collecting royalties on behalf of the author.

Offices in Canada, USA, UK, Ireland, and Spain
book sales for North America and international:
Trafford Publishing, 6E–2333 Government St.
Victoria, BC V8T 4P4 CANADA
phone 250 383 6864   toll-free 1 888 232 4444
fax 250 383 6804   email to orders@trafford.com
book sales in Europe:
Trafford Publishing (UK) Ltd., Enterprise House, Wistaston Road Business Centre
Crewe, Cheshire CW2 7RP UNITED KINGDOM
phone 01270 251 396   local rate 0845 230 9601
facsimile 01270 254 983   orders.uk@trafford.com '
order online at:
www.trafford.com/robots/04-0786.html

10   9   8   7   6

ACKNOWLEDGEMENTS

First of all I would like to thank my wife, Paulette, for supporting me on what might have appeared to be a hapless and thankless task, in particular her co-ordination of the administration. I would also like to thank my parents, Mr and Mrs Todd particularly for the early years which helped to form my character. I would also like to thank my son, Christopher, who inspired me by telling me about the behaviour of school and college boys on the streets. He opened my eyes to what the youth were doing on the streets. This worried me and prompted me to put pen to paper, as my contribution to the struggle. I thank my daughter Charlotte, not only for assisting me with abstract bits of information, but also for reminding me that when I am writing I am 'boring', in her words. The last point, in a sense, acts as a general reminder as to what life is all about. A special thanks to the rest of my family who, in their own inimitable way, helped support me through both illness and in health.

Also, special thanks to all those who helped me maintain the energy and those who contributed; Patsy Mckie of 'Mothers Against Violence. Lucy Cope, of Mothers' Against Gun Crime. Leslie Morrison, Head Teacher of a successful High School. Dee St-Lewis with regard to editorial support. Reverend McPherson of the Pentecostal City Mission Church Brixton and Christopher Todd for technical support and research.

Richard Anthony Todd

PREFACE

My parents arrived in the United Kingdom in 1954, some 9 years after the cessation of the Second World War. The only assets they had were youth, integrity and an honest belief in the virtues of hard work.

I was educated in an inner-London comprehensive school, which I left with only a few poorly graded CSEs. In brief, I have been through the complete United Kingdom education system and come out the other end with a story to tell that may assist others. I bring a level of subjectivity to issues that can only really be acquired by someone who has been through the system and, in doing so, gained first hand experience. Having said this, I have objectively analysed situations, which affect us as a wider community. The aim being not only to highlight the problems but also to offer recommendations or proposals, however distasteful those recommendations or proposals may be to society as a whole or to us as a community. Sometimes in life one has to take medicine, which is bitter and distasteful in order to overcome the ailment, which afflicts one's health. We, as a community, may need some medicine; it may be bitter, but it may just cure the ailments, which affect us. We must, therefore, brace ourselves in readiness to take whatever medicine is necessary and give it our full blessing, if it is going to have any healing or curing effect.

My career to date spans across 26 years of Public Sector service. In that time I have gained much experience and knowledge surrounding not only Public Sector issues, but also other business and social, issues. I have been involved in the property business for over 10 years now and, as such, have empirical knowledge of the economic and social problems besetting the Black community. Having said this, the main skill that I bring to this book is my ability to examine and evaluate a situation, and to report on weaknesses, along with drafting proposals where possible. Having been trained as an Internal Auditor to write reports for organisations about their systems of internal control, I have decided to use this skill to examine and evaluate where we are now as a community, (social audit). I am also a Co-opted Foundation Governor within a thriving inner-city school as well as a Financial Consultant to the Trustee Board of a church. I possess an MBA along with other accountancy and audit qualifications. I conclude with a strategic vision of the way forward for the community and, where appropriate, suggest proposals on how the Black community might achieve its goals. You may, or may not, agree with my reasoning or rationale; but, if it gets you talking and thinking about our plight, I will feel that the book has gone some way in raising the level of consciousness within our community.

My success criteria and hope, is that this book engenders a positive response, and brings about change for the better. Not just for us as individuals or even the community, but also for the wider society of which we are all a part. If any one individual is touched or moved by this book, I would consider it a success.

CONTENTS

CHAPTER I

INTRODUCTION

OVERALL AIMS AND OBJECTIVES OF THIS BOOK

The aim of this book is to outline where we are, as a Black community, with particular regard to education, heritage and our social standing. In order to do this, we must first understand where we came from and how we came to be here. To this end, the book outlines the West Indian journey to England, beginning with slavery and its impact on us today, with particular reference to the author's Jamaican origin, and his historical link with England.

This book seeks to establish whether the Black Community have a co-ordinated strategy or approach for dealing with Black-related issues or, at the very least want to be involved at a strategic level, with those organisations and institutions charged with developing and implementing policies pertaining to our community. This book does not go into detail on all aspects of Black-related issues, rather it brings together primary issues surrounding the plight of our community. This book does this by recording, where appropriate, the relevant empirical experience of the author, sharing not only his experience, but also his views and aspirations with you, the reader. It is hoped that some of the experiences delineated within this book will strike a chord with some of you, whilst others may find it eye opening.

When I use the term "community", I know that some of us may not be clear on exactly who the community is. Over the years, our community has changed. In the early years our community was readily identifiable, by colour and the fact that we were predominately from the West Indies. With the passage of time, this simplistic distinction no longer holds. As society itself has changed, so too has our community. The majority of us now are, in fact, UK born; others have come from other parts of the world, whilst some are of mixed race. It would now be fair to say that we have a plurality of identity. I am not a sociologist and, therefore, I will not give you a definition; but I am a pragmatist, and I know that we are held together by a common bond, because we suffer a common pain. That pain is a direct result of the negative effects of misplaced preconceptions and prejudice.

It is anticipated and hoped that this book will not only act as a catalyst for debate, but that it will also go some way towards providing the basis for a co-ordinated strategy, for dealing with the poignant issues facing our community.

Crime affects us all in one way or another; its effects on a community can be devastating. No economy can flourish, unless law and order is observed and preserved. Without the rule of law and order, no one has freedom. Communities where the crime rate is high will invariably suffer low levels of inward investment. Hence, there will be fewer jobs available to the local populous, a fact which, in itself, creates a downward spiral within the community. The economists refer to this downward spiral syndrome due to lack of investment as "The multiplier effect in reverse". The fear of crime is an attack on the quality of life of the law-abiding citizen. Some of our communities are being ravished by crime, or at least the threat of crime yet we, as a community, rarely talk about it let alone form strategies to combat it.

The lack of a good education could lead to a life of financial and social hardship. So many of our youngsters are not getting the kind of education that we as a community should expect. This will inevitably result in:

- An inability to compete in the labour market.
- Insufficient knowledge about business, and therefore inability to pursue an entrepreneurial career.

This book draws heavily on my experience, as a Black man born in the UK in the fifties to Jamaican parents. I feel a burning desire to contribute to the debate on education, crime and our status now, as a community within the United Kingdom. Where I feel it appropriate, I draw on my experience, in the honest belief that it is a microcosm of the wider problems affecting our community.

Throughout the book I use colloquial terms and phrases, where appropriate, in order to add poignancy and authenticity to the point I am making. In other areas I use poetry to convey a short, sharp and succinct message, in a way that will have impact and verve. Consequently, this is not a sociological study, researched at arms length by academics that have no real connection or feeling for what they are researching; quite the contrary is true. It is because I feel so passionate about my community that I feel the need to comment and share my experiences. I do this by trying to challenge you, confront you, inform you and even woo you.

It is in our interest and that of the wider society, that our multi-cultural society works. As such, we as a community must begin to look inwardly, to ask ourselves searching questions about our approach to life and where we fall in society as a whole. A type of SWOT (strengths, weaknesses, opportunities and threats) analysis, if you like, of where we are now as a community. For us to sit back, fold our arms and merely comment on the situation amongst our peer groups, is no longer a viable option. Inertia and apathy can never be a solution.

WHY I WROTE THIS BOOK

I went to the hospital for a routine check,
just thinking of my health that I so wanted to protect.
When one doctor consults another, you await your fate in horror.
He looked at my results with some concern,
I was so nervous my tummy began to churn.
For I was not prepared for what I was about to learn.

"Sir I am sorry bad news, you have a problem with your left kidney,"
I exclaimed, "how can that be I came in here healthy".
The Doctor then went on to say, " the good news is you're in the right place,"
he went on to say, "there is no time to waste lets make haste."
My mind became void of thought and feeling,
from the floor I looked to the clean blue ceiling.

All my plans for the future were now on hold,
my whole body went freezing cold.
I was consumed in the depths of despair,
I could see my future dangling there.
Was I going to live or die?
Why me, I thought, as I gazed to the sky.
How could the Doctor say I was a lucky guy,
Whilst I was in denial thinking it was an ugly lie.

The Surgeon's smile stood me in good stead for a while,
but when I was alone, I thought was this something I have to face on my own?
However the family was steadfastly there,
I give thanks for their support and, unfettered care,
perhaps that is the reason in part why I am still here.

My fate was in the Surgeon's hand,
my destiny was no longer mine as a man,
I thought to myself at that low point, what is the meaning of life?
Why did I go through all that toil and strife?
If this is the sum total of my life,
to end up under the Surgeons knife?
Life is so strange when you are staring into the abyss,
life throws up the most unusual twists.

I thought to myself, if I recover I have to write,
about some of the issues that we face as a community and our plight.

I remembered one African Chief (accountant) giving me a funny look,
he said , "Richard my son, you are going to write a book."
He said, believe what I am telling you.
You will see that it will come true.
To be honest I thought he did not have a clue,
but what have we here in front of you.

This is how I came to write this book,
I implore all of you to have a look.
Some say the Lord has graciously spoken,
others say my talent has just awoken.
Whatever your point of view,
This book has something for all of you!

Richard Todd

BACKGROUND

We as a Black West Indian community have been in the United Kingdom for over 50 years. In that time there have been some notable successes. Sports personalities have done extremely well, others have done well in the music and other industries. However, the main success was indeed the original West Indians, who arrived here in the 1950's. They worked hard, they purchased their own homes, they raised their families. Given their humble origins, and the difficulties they faced when they first arrived, their achievements have been no less than astounding. We should respect them and thank them, for they prepared the way for future generations to move forward.

Somewhere along the line we have lost the focus and lost the plot. Instead of taking the baton and running with it, we have dropped it and, in some cases we refuse to pick it up. This book looks back as well as forward in a bid to assess where we are now as a community. Consequently the book begins by examining our past, with particular regard to slavery and the effects that slavery may still have on us, years after its abolition.

Black on Black crime has now reached an all time high within the UK. The (January 2003) killings in Birmingham where young women were fatally shot, was a tragic, yet poignant reminder of where we are now. The teenage girls were at a party enjoying themselves when tragedy struck in a brutal way. Gunmen opened fire in a cold and callous way; gangster style. Yet throughout 2003 the senseless killings continued consistently and relentlessly. We, as a community, rarely discuss crime and general anti-social behaviour. The rare few times we do discuss it, we do not appear to move towards a consensus, let alone develop a strategy to deal with the problem. It is futile to keep discussing crime within our community without moving towards a definitive plan of action. If our community has no clear approach on how to deal with crime and anti social-behaviour within our community, why then should we feel hurt if other institutions and communities impose a solution upon us?

Time after time you will hear reporters talk about what is happening on our streets and now, even the Black churches are taking a stand. The churches are now going out on the street, at night, confronting disenfranchised young men and pointing out the error of their ways, whilst offering prayer and spiritual guidance. We have also heard distinguished Black leaders stress the need for education amongst the youth; whilst at the same time other community leaders are simply in denial regarding Black crime.

The so-called "bad man" culture is prevalent amongst our young men. Some men walk around with faces that reflect anger, the so-called "screw face" syndrome. An urban expression to signify street aggression which, in effect, staves off would-be predators but, at the same time, intimidates vulnerable individuals within the community.

The book takes a candid look at the effects of some government policies and their application, via public sector institutions and organisations, on the Black community.

The Black community is over represented in the penal system and under represented in the Criminal Justice System (CJS). Furthermore, there is a general lack of understanding about what the CJS is and how it works. This book outlines the workings of the system, and details the component parts of the CJS.

Black boys have one of the lowest levels of educational attainment across all the racial groups. The implication of this in the longer term for us as a community is alarming. Exclusions from school, particularly amongst black boys, have reached an all time high. It therefore follows that if these boys fall out of the educational system, their employment opportunities will be blighted; they may join the ranks of the criminal fraternity. It is, indeed, what I refer to as 'the nightmare scenario'. There is an old saying "An hungry man is an angry man" An uneducated, disenfranchised, young man is a dangerous man. The challenge for us as a community is to recognise this and break the cycle of poor education.

This book touches on issues surrounding mental health care within our community. As such the author seeks to explore the short comings, not only in the health institutions that provide services for the mentally impaired, but in our attitude as a community. In addition there is commentary on the following;

1. Breakdown of the family.
2. Our attitude to money.
3. Work.
4. Business and business concepts, such as communication with each other.
5. Leadership
6. The church.

CHAPTER II

THE SLAVE TRADE

INTRODUCTION

Sometimes, in order to assess where we are now, as a people, we must examine where we are coming from.

Our West Indian history begins with the slave trade. Although slavery had been a feature of human life since as early as 2,600 B.C. in Egypt, it became an extremely lucrative European trade in the late fifteenth century. It did not take Britain long to cash in on the trade in human beings. Ships left British west coast ports such as; Liverpool and Bristol, laden with firearms, gunpowder, metals, alcohol, cotton goods, beads, knives and mirrors, the sort of things which African chiefs desired, but did not have. These commodities were often of very poor quality. Many of these inferior goods were made in Birmingham and were known as "Brummagem ware". These goods were exchanged for slaves, people who had been captured in local tribal wars perhaps, or who had been taken prisoner especially for this trade.

The ships and their crews were independent operators who in today's world would probably be called independent, unregulated contractors. They took advantage of the opportunity to provide African Chiefs with European products of its 'civilisation' in return for human beings. It was indeed a form of conflict between capitalism and morality. The worrying thing was that capitalism won the battle then and perhaps in some cases it still does now.

THE MIDDLE PASSAGE

The terrible transformation of the 17th to the 19th Century, tells of the largest forced migration in recorded history and how this mass movement of people was instrumental in the creation of the British & North American colonies. After establishing settlements in North America, England joined Spain, Portugal, and the Netherlands in the international trade in human beings. Millions of Africans were abducted from their homelands, to labour in the North American and British colonies. So horrific was their "middle passage" across the Atlantic that almost a quarter of them died during the crossing. The human cargo was packed like sardines. From a management perspective, losing a quarter of one's stock in the transport stage would indeed be a poor show, as profits would therefore be reduced; but slaves were cheap and expendable.

SICK SLAVES

One afternoon I was examining my daughter's homework, it touched upon slavery. My daughter drew my attention to one anecdotal story, about a female African slave, who whilst on a transport ship called "Moonlight" fell ill with fever. She was unceremoniously thrown overboard; for fear that she would infect the other slaves. Sick slaves, of course, represented lower profit margins, and ship owners would not allow profit margins to be compromised. This is only one story, but can you imagine for a minute how many times that would have happened, tens of thousands perhaps, given the appalling conditions in which they were transported.

BRANDING AND CHAINING SLAVES

Upon their arrival, families who survived the trip would be separated and sent to various masters usually, plantation owners. They were bound and branded like property or chattel. Yes you've guessed it, even woman were chained like beasts. Sometimes the less said, the better; this is such a time.

SPRINGBOARD FOR NEW WORLD COLONIALISM

Barbados, in many respects, was England's first experimental tropical agricultural export colony, and was successful for a number of related reasons. Contemporary opinion of the late 17th Century acclaimed it the richest spot of ground in the world. Private English capital, with the Crown's blessing, financed settlement in 1627. Market conditions for its first commercial crop, tobacco, enabled the accumulation of quick profits. These profits were later utilised to finance the shift to sugar production in the 1650s, after large scale, high quality Virginian tobacco production caused a glut on the European market and prices to plummet. Barbados quickly acquired the largest white population of any of the English colonies in the so-called New World, (American continent). In many respects, Barbados became the springboard for English colonisation in the New World, playing a leading role in the settlement of Jamaica and the Carolinas and sending a constant flow of settlers to other areas throughout the 17th and early 18th centuries. Even today, many still refer to Barbados as 'Little England'. This gave rise to the transatlantic slave trade, which was organised on a three-point circuit and was commonly referred to as the **'triangular trade'**. Risks were high but, on a 'good' voyage, a profit could be made at each point of the triangular trade.

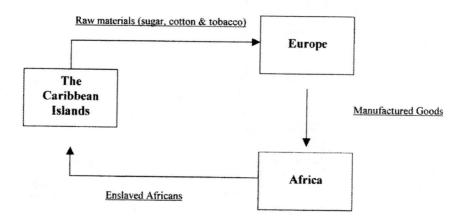

THE PROFIT MOTIVE

In the West Indian colonies, Europeans relied on Africans' skills and labour to transform vast areas of land into profit making agricultural concerns. The sheer brutality of the regime was not something well documented, as the slaves at that time were illiterate; nor was it in the interest of the slave masters to document what they were doing. The slave masters made great profits. In a purely economic sense; if an organisation or country can obtain free labour, then the cost of production will be vastly reduced. It was this simple, capitalistic, doctrine that gave rise to slavery. Trinidadian historian, Eric Williams, showed in his well-researched book "Capitalism and Slavery", that the slave trade and slavery, helped to make England 'the workshop of the world'. Profits from slave-worked colonies and the slave trade were major sources of capital accumulation, which helped finance the industrial revolution. It was during the years of slave trade and slavery that Whites affirmed their superiority over Blacks. It is not difficult to understand why white traders, who bought Black people for the price of adulterated brandy and packed them onto slave ships like cattle, could consider themselves to be superior. Though most were illiterate, crude, and drunken, white slave traders were free men, herding flocks of human cattle. As the centuries passed, Europeans became more and more scornful of Black people. By the 19th Century, various theories of Black inferiority were developed and used, in part, to justify the colonisation of Africa.

THE ROLE OF BRISTOL CITY IN THE SLAVE TRADE

The City of Bristol played a major part in the transatlantic slave trade of the 17th and 18th Centuries. In memory of the tens of thousands of slaves taken from West Africa to the Caribbean and on board the Bristol ships, Bristol City Council Leisure Services set up the Bristol Slave Trade Action Group (BSTG). The group aims to raise awareness of Bristol's slave trading past and find ways of acknowledging Bristol's part in the trade.

HORRORS OF SLAVERY

However, with so little written documentation to refer to, art is perhaps the best possible historical record, made by those who were there, at the so-called sharp end. If a picture speaks a thousand words then let the facts speak for themselves. The common theme of most of the art shows slaves shackled and being beaten, and very often half naked.

Our forefathers were taken forcibly, from their homelands in Western Africa, to shores far away. They were led like lambs to the slaughter, yet they opened not their mouths; to have done so would have led to certain extinction. The West Indies, as we know it now would never have existed. Slaves who attempted to abscond were hunted down and punished in the most heinous fashion. In many cases one of their feet would be severed, so they would never run again, in other cases they were lashed with a whip until they bled, salt and pepper would then be rubbed into thier wounds.

SLAVE AUTOBIOGRAPHY

The power of the written word has longevity. Therefore any slave that could record the plight of slavery was a rarity and therefore precious. Olaudah Equiano composed the first ever slave autobiography, as a freed slave living in England. His autobiography, 'The Life of Gustavus Vassa' (Gustavus Vassa was one of the names given to him by his owners), became a phenomenal best seller in its time, both in England and America. It fuelled a young but growing anti-slavery movement. Equiano narrates his life from boyhood onwards. He was born in an African village in the Gold-Coast, sold into slavery to another village, moved to yet another village as a slave and finally captured and sold to European slavers. Outlined below is an extract of his account in his own Victorian English grammatical style:

While my master thus employed me, I was often a witness to cruelties of every kind, which were exercised on my unhappy fellow slaves. I used frequently to have different cargoes of new Negroes in my care for sale; and it was almost a constant practice with our clerks, and other whites, to commit violent depredations on the chastity of the female slaves; and these I was, though with reluctance, obliged to submit to at all times, being unable to help them. When we have had some of these slaves on board my master's vessel, to carry them to other islands, or to America, I have known oar mates to commit these acts most shamefully, to the disgrace, not of Christians only, but of men. I have even known them gratify their brutal passion with females not ten years old; and these abominations, some of them practiced to such scandalous excess, that one of our captains discharged the mate and others on that account. And yet in Montserrat I have seen a negro man staked to the ground, and cut most shockingly, and then his ears cut off bit by bit, because he had been connected with a white woman, who was a common prostitute. As if it were no crime in the whites to rob an innocent African girl of her virtue; but most heinous in a black man only to gratify a passion of nature, where the temptation was offered by one of a different colour, though the most abandoned woman of her species.

Equiano also records his central role, along with others, in the British Abolitionist Movement. As a major voice in this movement, Equiano petitioned the Queen of England in 1788. He was appointed commissary of provisions and stores to the expedition to resettle London's poor Blacks in Sierra Leone, a British colony on the west coast of Africa.

DIVIDE AND RULE

One way in which slave masters controlled their slaves was by depriving them of education. Slaves were forbidden to learn to read or write; in other words they were denied basic education. To keep a people illiterate was to keep them weak and subordinate to their White slave masters. They knew then, as we know now, that true freedom could only come through education. Even after the abolition of slavery, it took years for real freedom to come, as freed slaves were illiterate and, mentally, still in chains. In the 17th and 18th centuries African slaves who spoke the same language were kept separate, to prevent slave revolts. This meant that English became the slaves' common language. The slaves consequently used a language of English and West African linguistics. This gave rise to local pidgin languages which were developed, in the slave territories. Pidgins are marginal languages created by people who need to communicate, but have no common language. Jamaican pidgin (patois) originated in this way, however, Jamaica is essentially an English speaking Country.

It was great to see English rugby hiting an all time high, the national team having won the world cup in 2003. It was lovely to hear all the supporters cheering and singing the theme song "Swing low, sweet chariot", but were did that originate from? Just listen to some of the words:

Swing low, sweet chariot
Comin' for to carry me home
Swing low, sweet chariot
Comin' for to carry me home
I looked over Jordan and what did I see
Comin' for to carry me home
A band of angels comin' after me
Comin' for to carry me home

"Swing Low, Sweet Chariot" along with "We Shall Overcome," "Deep River," was sung by the slaves as they hungered for escape to freedom and an end to enslavement, as well as interpreting and teaching the ancient biblical stories of courage and salvation. Generally when I hear these songs, I have an innate sense of sadness, a sense of foreboding if you like; but I felt the same before I knew these songs were linked to slavery. These spirituals have become part of the very fabric of global Christianity today.

Thankfully, we may never know the full graphic horrors of slavery, but just imagine; families torn apart; child taken from mother, husband parted from wife; and women used as sex objects and concubines. There was also a forced breeding programme, where strong young Black men would be made to have sexual intercourse with healthy Black females, a process designed to produce strong offspring and, therefore, greater profits for their masters. Need I say any more? The question that I would ask is this, "Does that sort of interbreeding of the fittest of the fittest and the strongest of the strongest, create a physical thoroughbred. Could this be the reason why descendants of slaves excel so much at sport, where speed and power are of the essence? Food for thought don't you think?"

Today we still see the lack of education and dysfunctional Black families as major issues within our community. The question I would ask is this, do our current problems surrounding education and dysfunctional families have their roots firmly planted in the days of the slave trade"?

MY TANGIBLE LINK TO SLAVERY

On my first trip to Jamaica, as a teenager, I asked my Grandmother about slavery. She pondered on the question for some time, before telling me that her grandmother was born a slave and, remained a slave up until the age of nine. This took me by surprise, because I then realised that I had a tangible link within my ancestry to slavery. It was no longer something that related to someone else, this was my history and, therefore, my reality. This was no longer an abstract history lesson; rather it formed part of the core of my very being. The horror of slavery weighs heavily on our shoulders and could be responsible in part for our consumerist attitude today. The effects of hundreds of years of slavery may still be in our sub-conscious. Our forefathers would turn in their graves if they could see us now. They would not believe in their wildest dreams that we would be here today. The opportunities that we have open to us now are clear to see for those with the vision to see them.

EMANCIPATION

Abolition of slavery was to come from an unlikely source. You probably wouldn't have chosen the young Wilberforce as a moral crusader. Only five feet tall and rather homely, by most accounts, William Wilberforce had a smooth and powerful way of speaking. It wasn't easy, but this Christian politician managed to talk the British Empire into abolishing slavery. He was born into a wealthy family and would have enjoyed the pleasures that slavery brought. Slavery was one of those hidden scandals, comfortably out of sight of the average Englishman, who benefited from it but never had to see firsthand the unspeakable human misery. Through the influence of Newton and others, Wilberforce knew what he had to do.

From the 17th Century until the 19th Century, almost twelve million Africans were brought to the New World against their will, to perform backbreaking labour under terrible conditions. After 1830, when the mood of the nation changed in favour of a variety of reforms, the anti-slavery campaign gathered momentum. Slavery was abolished on 1st August 1834, although illegal slave trading continued for decades after. Wilberforce, on his deathbed, was informed of the passing of the Act in the nick of time. The main terms of the Act were:

1. All slaves under the age of six were to be freed immediately.
2. Slaves over the age of six were to remain as part slave and part free for a further four years. In that time they would have to be paid a wage for the work they did in the quarter of the week when they were "free".
3. The government was to provide £20 million in compensation to the slave-owners who had lost their "property".

Therein lay one of the biggest absurdities ever recorded. The oppressor was rewarded for relinquishing control of the oppressed to the tune of £20 million. (Billions in today's money) Those who suffered i.e. the slaves were never compensated.

Wilberforce was to die but a few short days later, having spent most of his adult life fighting and championing the battle to free the slaves. Wilberforce's success does however, beg the question as to where the church was whilst the slave trade prospered for hundreds of years?

In the West Indies, the economic results after the Emancipation Act were disastrous. The islands depended on the sugar trade, which in turn depended on slave labour. Ultimately, the planters were unable to continue to make the West Indies the thriving centres of trade which they had been in the eighteenth century. The abolition of slavery did not mean the cessation of subordination; in a sense the subordination continued until well into the 19th century. Ships carrying slaves could be intercepted and the ship owner fined £100 for each slave found on board. When intercepted by the Royal Navy, the shipmaster would order the slaves to be thrown overboard to avoid paying the fine.

COLONY OF THE BRITISH EMPIRE

As little as 80 years ago we were still subordinate to the, then colonial, masters. We may have had a certain amount of liberty, but we did not have self-determination. This type of ingrained control over generations of people still has an impact on us to this day.

The oxford dictionary defines a colony as a territory belonging to a state by conquest or annexation. Since the abolition of slavery, we toiled under the weight of colonialism in the West Indies. Even though many West Indian Islands became independent in the 1960's, poverty and deprivation in the region still remain widespread.

So many slaves (and subsequently British subjects) made the ultimate sacrifice for the 'Mother Land', they worked, they toiled, they fought and they died for Great Britain. Perhaps now is the time, in this age of enlightenment and knowledge, for this to be recognised; not just by us as a community but also by the wider society.

INHUMANITY

Man's inhumanity to man was demonstrated without conscience during the period of the slave trade. The dehumanisation and degradation of Africans as a people, in the pursuit of profit and personal gratification, is an abhorrence of the highest order. However, supporters of the trade at that time claimed that it was not inhumane, that they were acting in the slaves' interest.

We should not forget this integral part of our history, nor should we allow it to hold us back, or colour our judgement about the way forward. We know we have been the victims of a grave and inhumane injustice but, equally, we know the only way forward is through reconciliation. Suffice to say, some of us behave as though we are still in the aftermath of slavery, some 170 years after slavery was abolished. Carnival, 'partying' and now in an indirect way, 'raving' derives from rejoicing after emancipation. Are we now still in 'aftershock' and is this the reason why we see 'raving' and 'partying' as such an important aspect of our social agenda? The Black Community, are renowned for our bubbly parties and clubs and our nimble footwork on the dance floor. In contrast, we are not known for business acumen or academic thinking. It is perhaps quite apt that I should now quote the late Robert Nester Marley, *"emancipate yourself from mental slavery, none but ourselves can free up our minds"*. Further to this, I would suggest that anyone who has the opportunity of an education but does not attempt to take it, is not only letting themselves down, but also their community and their ancestors, who knew nothing other than the pain of toil.

SOUTH AFRICAN APARTHEID

In recent times we have seen the cessation of apartheid in South Africa and, in Nelson Mandela we see a living legend. A man who gave up freedom and liberty in order to further the struggle against injustice and oppression. He was imprisoned for 26 years by a brutal regime, but yet he bares no ill will to those that were the cause of his suffering. In fact, Nelson Mandela brought about a relatively peaceful revolution, in that he brought true democracy and liberty to his people. Nelson Mandela's sphere of influence does not begin and end in South Africa, but it is an inspiration to mankind the world over.

The South African Truth and Reconciliation Commission (TRC) was set up by the South African Government of National Unity, to help deal with what happened under apartheid. The conflict during this period resulted in violence and human rights abuse perpetrated; in the main, by those forces who were an integral part of the apartheid regime. No section of society escaped. The TRC was about bringing the oppressors during apartheid face to face with the families of their victims. The aim was for the perpetrators to explain their actions. It was a painful experience for the victims and many families who lost loved ones. Many families learned for the first time when and how their loved ones were killed. Yet in a strange way it was the beginning of the healing process, it was a point of reconciliation.

Nelson Mandela knew that if people harbour hate in their hearts, there can never be peace.

NO TRUTH AND RECONCILIATION COMMISSION FOR SLAVERY VICTIMS

Those who survived the Middle Passage were forced to work day and night for masters who knew no mercy, just for the right to stay alive. We lost our religion, language, self esteem, culture and our freedom to determine our own destiny, yet we survived. Where therefore was our Truth and Reconciliation Commission? The reality is we never had a TRC or anything like it. With the passing of time the option of a TRC is no longer possible, as those responsible have long since died. Therefore we have not really had the opportunity to heal our wounds in the same way as Nelson Mandela managed for his people. We never really hear the slave trade discussed these days by politicians or the mass media, it is a mere footnote in British history, still it is at the core of our history. After all, it is not yet 170 years since slavery was formerly abolished. The Jewish holocaust by contrast is well documented, quite rightly so, and it acts as testimony to man's inhumanity towards his fellow man. If we do not learn the lessons of history, of what prejudice and hate can lead to, do we not run the risk of history repeating itself?

LESSON LEARNED

There is a real lesson to be learned from the TRC for us as a community; it is the lesson of reconciliation, and love for mankind. As you will read in this book, I have personally had negative experiences at the hands of individuals and institutions, but I do not harbour hate or bad feeling. Mankind, throughout history, has acted with unspeakable wickedness and evil towards fellow man for one reason or another. Many of you who read this will be able to identify with what I am saying. Notwithstanding this, I use the negativity of the past to give me strength for the future. Nonetheless it is imperative that we, as a community, begin to know, understand and realise where we are coming from, because it is not until we know where we are coming from that we are able to gauge where we are going. It is not helpful for us to focus on the evils of the past; rather we should plan for the good of the future.

DID WE EVER GET OUR FREE PAPERS

I recall an old Jamaican saying that my parents use to say when school holidays were finished "*Your free paper burn*", which means, your free abandonment has come to an end, as a new school term is about to begin. This was synonymous with slaves who were freed having to demonstrate their freedom with a document which they should carry on their persons at all times. The question I would ask, however, is this; "Have we exchanged one form of slavery for another? Did we really ever receive our free paper? Or are we still running around like long lost sheep, whose lost their master and has gone astray?"

PRESIDENT BUSH'S STATEMENT

President Bush and the First Lady arrived in South Africa in July 2003 for the second stop on their tour of Africa. President Bush's daughter, Barbara, was on the trip as well. They were in Senegal before visiting the South African capital of Pretoria. They continued on to Botswana, Uganda and Nigeria, all allies in the US war on terrorism. In Senegal, Bush visited Goree Island, where hundreds of thousands of Africans were once bought and sold. Bush saw the dungeon-like cells where many were kept in misery and chains. Bush called it "very moving" and, said in a speech afterwards that "the United States is still struggling with the legacy of slavery". Bush spoke of redemption and the triumph of the human spirit as he recalled; "one of the largest migrations of history." He went on to say "By a plan known only to Providence, the stolen sons and daughters of Africa helped to awaken the conscience of America. The very people traded into slavery helped to set America free".

Africana.com, an online magazine, first published the above summary in May 2003.

FUTURE

The Hon. Marcus Garvey, a great Jamaican Orator, once said; "I do not speak carelessly or recklessly but with a definite object of helping the people, especially those of my race, *to know, to understand, and to realize themselves.*" Those words still ring true today, some 80 years after they were first uttered.

One final thought for you to consider; without knowledge of our past, how can we set out our road map, as it were, for the future? If we do not know where we are coming from, then how do we know where we are going to? If we don't know who we are, then how do we know who we want to be? The future is for those who prepare for it and if we keep both eyes on the past, we will not be prepared for the future.

FROM SLAVERY TO BRAVERY

One final thought for you to contemplate,
Look how long slavery took to abate,
It seems to me that some of us are still confused,
and others refuse to be enthused.

Wake up my friend, from your deep slumber,
it is our time now to remember.
Hundreds of years of unadulterated slavery,
and the sheer brutality, only matched by our forefathers' bravery.

We cannot and should not forget our past,
but we must forgive and move forward in a way that will last.
It is because we suffered a great inhumanity,
why we should come together in love and humility.

As Martin Luther King Jnr. stated, "I do not know what the future holds,
but I do know who holds the future".

Richard Todd

THE SLAVERY IN ME

I have no hate in my heart,
but let's get it straight from the start.
You say that everything evil is Blacker than Black.
You say that everything that is pure and good is Whiter than White,
but how on earth could that be right?
Was it not the White man,
that enslaved the African?
This part of history you choose to forget,
but not much remorse do I detect.

You took as a slave one who was born a free African,
and turned him into an African American or West Indian.
Yet you never thought it was wrong,
that's why you continued this trade for so long.

Four hundred years of slavery is a long time,
perhaps it says something about mankind.
Slavery lasted for sixteen or more generations,
to date we have seen no reparations.

You tore husbands from wives,
and forced each to live separate slave lives.
You tore children away from mothers,
you tore sisters away from brothers.
You committed unspeakable horror,
at the time you showed no sorrow.

You murdered runaway slaves at will.
You murdered slaves who just did not fit the bill.
You hunted slaves merely to kill.
You watched slaves fight each other just for the thrill.

Some you amputated limb by limb,
others you treated equally as grim.
Was this not a crime against humanity,
or was this another example of mans insanity?

I told you from the start,
that I have no hate in my heart.
Man must love their fellow man,
it is all part of the Almighty plan.

When you see me on the street today,
Think about what happened to me and mine yester year,
if you dare and if you care.
Think for a minute, about where I am coming from,
you must see now, that in my past, I have been totally wronged.

Richard Todd

CHAPTER III

MY HERITAGE

INTRODUCTION

Not many people have either the time or opportunity to chart their ancestry. My sister, who showed energy and drive, decided to do just that as she embarked upon the dusty trail of mapping out the family history. Through a series of contacts and with the blessed Internet, she managed to trace the family tree back to 1530, which took us deep into middle England. Ostensibly, I am a product of two separate and yet distinct cultures:

- Slave Trade
- Middle Class England

The slave trade by its very definition made it difficult, if not impossible, to trace family ancestry with regard to Africa as so little was documented. Perhaps those that could have documented it had a vested interest in not documenting their deeds. On the other hand, my English ancestry is documented and, therefore, it can and has been traced.

To understand ourselves as a people, we must acquaint ourselves with the past, just as African slavery is an integral part of our being, so is our European connection. I have dedicated a whole chapter to slavery, as it strikes at the core of our very being but, in the interest of completeness, I have explored my White English ancestry also.

ENGLISH ANCESTRY

Many Jamaicans have ancestral links with England, and I believe that my story is a macrocosm of that situation. Until recently I have had little knowledge of my ancestry, beyond my Grandfather, who died around the same time that I was born. Many West Indians today will have direct biological links to Slave Masters of the past. Others will have been the offspring of interracial relationships.

THOMAS TODD 1530 TO 1600

In 1530, Thomas Todd was born in Durham, a quintessential English man; he was later to become a clergyman of good standing. I will not go into detail about the chain of events which led the Todds to Jamaica, but what I will ask is this, "Is this not another reason as to why we have a moral and ethical right to be in England?" The fact that I still bear his name, hundreds of years later, is astounding and, at the same time a gentle reminder of our historical links with England. Some may say it's providence, others will say its coincidence, whatever your point of view is, the fact remains that there is a European connection to us of Afro-Caribbean descent that can not be denied much the same way that our link to slavery is irrefutable.

Thomas Todd

JAMAICA

Jamaica, the land of my forefathers, is an independent Country in the Caribbean and a member of the British Commonwealth of Nations, located south of Cuba and west of Haiti in the Caribbean Sea. Jamaica is the third largest island of the Greater Antilles.

Christopher Columbus learned of Jamaica from the indigenous people on the island of Cuba, during his second voyage to the New World (Americas). He set foot on the northern part of Jamaica, at present-day Saint Ann's Bay, on 4th May, 1494.

Spain sent Juan de Esquivel to establish a settlement in 1509, thus began Spain's effective colonisation of Jamaica. The Spanish established Sevilla la Nueva, on the northern part of the island, as their first administrative centre but abandoned it in 1523 for Saint Jago de la Vega (now Spanish Town) in the south.

On 10th May, 1655, an English expedition, commanded by Admiral William Penn and General Robert Venables, landed at the present-day coastal town of Passage Fort, in the southeastern parish of Saint Catherine. This expedition, which had failed to capture Hispaniola, proceeded to claim the island of Jamaica for England. They were met with limited resistance and quickly overwhelmed the island.

THE CALL TO SUPPORT THE 'MOTHERLAND'

Out of a colonial (Caribbean) population of 14 million in the British Commonwealth, about 16,000 West Indians volunteered for service alongside the British during the Second World War. Of these, well over a 100 were women. Posted overseas 80 chose the WAAF (Women's Auxiliary Air Force) as their contribution, whilst around 30 joined the ATS (Auxiliary Territorial Service).

Around 6,000 West Indians served with the Royal Air Force and the Royal Canadian Air Force, in roles from fighter pilots to bomb aimers, air gunners to ground staff and administration. Thousands of West Indian seamen made their contribution in one of the Second World War's most dangerous services, the Merchant Navy – one third of all merchant seamen were to die during the war.

After the Second World War, in 1945, at the behest and request of Sir Winston Churchill, West Indians made the torrid journey to the "Mother Land" (England) as it was referred to at the time. The West Indian came here to help restore a country that had been ravished during the war by providing much needed labour for the public sector and industry. We now refer to the first West Indians that arrived in the UK after the war as "the first generation". It had taken some degree of courage in those days to leave the safety of one's community and family and travel by ship, thousands of miles over many weeks, to an unknown destiny. But come they did. If one compares this to today's world, with better communications and transport, the same journey would take a matter of hours.

MIGRATION TO BRITAIN

The 'Public Record Office' web site recorded the following:

Immediately after the Second World War, on the 'MV Empire Windrush' many West Indians who had seen war service in the UK returned here in search of better career opportunities. A few years later, on 22 June 1948, the first big group of people from the Caribbean (492 in all) arrived at Tilbury Docks in London seeking employment. Although the British Government had been discussing the possibility of using surplus colonial labour to meet demand, it was alarmed by such a large and unexpected contingent. As British citizens, they had the right to live and work in Britain. Yet they came up against considerable opposition from local people, especially when trying to find accommodation and good jobs. Due to an accommodation problem, the Colonial Office was forced to house 230 settlers in a deep air raid shelter in Clapham Common. The nearest labour exchange happened to be in Brixton, which therefore became one of Britain's first West Indian communities.

Hence, the late 1940s marked the beginning of West Indian (British Citizens) migration to Britain. Naturally, when they arrived they moved to urban areas in which the need for labour was most prevalent. Many of the new arrivals were not prepared for the indifferent response they got from the host nation but, with fortitude and determination, they worked and overcame those obstacles. Some came with the intention to return in a few short years, others had longer-term aspirations. Getting accommodation was difficult and long working hours for small pay was the norm. So began the West Indian ethnic communities within the UK.

It is important to note, from the point of historical correctness that some Black communities already existed here, in areas such as Liverpool and Cardiff.

OUT OF THE SUNSHINE TO THE COLD EMPLOYMENT LINE

Out of the tropical splendour of the Caribbean sunshine,
they left their loved ones and waved them goodbye for the last time.
Some they would never see again,
whilst others would always remain a pen pal friend.
The call for labour from the Motherland, was so great,
as British Subjects, they had no time to abate, or wait.

So the story begins, the story of the West Indian migration.
A story that begins on the shoreline of the Caribbean.
The descendants of whom are now born European.
They came here at the request and behest,
of, none other than, Sir Winston Churchill, no less.
Some of the story remains yet untold,
we will see over the next few years how the story unfolds.

A journey that would take weeks by ship,
it was a long and arduous trip.
They had great expectation of the victorious Motherland,
but they were apprehensive about what they might face, on the other hand.

When the English shoreline came into sight, at first light,
they knew they had reached England, and so would begin their plight.
The weather was grey, foggy, and cold, it was truly dismal,
with snow on the ground and dampness all around, some say it was abysmal.
In the cold and damp, chimneys would bellow smoke,
was this nightmare for real they thought, or was it a silly joke?
This was surely not the Great Britain they learned about at school,
as they recapped, the Motherland was there in order to rule.

The first problem they faced was getting somewhere to stay,
no Blacks, no Irish and no dogs, was the order of the day.
How could they have been treated in this awful way?
but they were determined to stay, come what may.
In many cases there were three or four occupants in one room,
But it was not always doom and gloom.
They knew that over the arising, greater things loomed.

No time to waste, immediately they went down to the labour exchange,
that was the only way to earn a little change.

They came here to work, they did not come here to shirk.
they did not come to hide or lurk,
all they wanted was a job of work.
They worked for long hours and low pay,
nothing came to them on a tray.
They sent some of what little money the yearned back home,
to the old folks left alone,
along with an airmail letter to say "How are you".
It was hard, but really the folk back home, did not have a clue.

At the first opportunity they brought their houses,
others sent back home for their spouses.
Some wanted to earn enough and go back home,
others wanted to make England their home.
Some wanted to afford their children greater opportunity,
others wanted to be free to work with impunity.

The world is a much smaller place nowadays,
and things have changed in so many ways.
So when I look at the first generation, I see pioneer.
When I look at the first generation, I see some as debonair.
When I look at the first generation I see voyagers without fear.
When I look at the first generation I see those that brought us here.

This is why we have to care,
they made a pathway for us, that is now, all too clear.
It is for us to grace what they did yesterday,
with the respect they deserve today.

Richard Todd

BEAUTIFUL JAMAICA

The 'Jamaican Gleaner' states on its web page that if "Jamaica, were compared to a painting it would be a masterpiece of tropical splendour". Framed by towering Blue Mountains, the landscape is filled with the multi-coloured hues of exotic flowers and plants and subdued by the various greens of dense jungles, woody meadows and misty valleys. Countless waterfalls tumble and cascade downward, over boulders and gorges, feeding the rivers which spread out like hundreds of fingers across the island. I defy anyone that has travelled to Jamaica to suggest that it is anything other than beautiful.

Behind the mosaic beauty that typifies the landscape of Jamaica, there lies the stark reality of poverty, social deprivation and crime. Some of the houses in Jamaica are exquisite and would compare with good houses anywhere else in the world but they all have one common denominator, the infamous burglar bars. This in itself speaks volumes about the level of crime in Jamaica, along with the excessive use of dogs, not as pets, but as working guard dogs. However, this is not only true of Jamaica, other countries have similar problems but because Jamaica is the land from which I originate, I feel compelled to comment.

MY JAMAICAN REALITY CHECK

My first trip to Jamaica as a teenager was a reality check; I saw poverty co-existing with opulence. The question I had to ask myself was "where do I fit?". The infrastructure and educational system that I had taken for granted in the UK, at that time became all the more important to me. This brings to mind an old Jamaican proverb " *Want it, want it, can't get it, and get it, get it, don't want it*". When said in the local vernacular, it has a ring to it which is lost in the written word. The message it conveys is "Those that have access to opportunity don't always take the opportunity, and those who do not have this access crave it". When one sees an adult living in a zinc shed three meters square and others living in homes that far exceed their needs, it focuses the mind on the harsh realities of the world. The trip brought home to me how pervasive poverty can be, how it stifles opportunity. That trip was to change my attitude forever. I was shocked to the core, but, in a strange way, it was to force me to examine my own achievement, or lack of achievement, at that time. Where would I fit in the scheme of things? Would I be one of those that 'have' or one of those who 'have not', and I came to the conclusion that if I was not cautious I would swell the ranks of the 'have nots'. It then dawned upon

me that when I returned to the UK, I needed to do something and I
needed to do it quickly.

WHY LEAVE JAMAICA?

Some years later, I was on holiday in Discovery Bay, Jamaica, in a
seaside villa which was built into the rocky shoreline overlooking the
clear blue Caribbean Sea.

It was simply majestic. Every morning I sat in the villa watching
the tide caress the base of rocky shoreline, the cool sea breeze em-
braced my body. It was a heavenly experience, unlike any other. I
then began to ask myself a question. "If Jamaica is so beautiful then
why would my parents and many like them, want to leave the undeniable splendour? what was the driving force behind such a drastic
decision"?

The answer was to come from a strange, yet poignant, source but
come it did. As we visited my late grandmother who was well over
ninety years old, I jokingly asked my daughter "who lives here"? To
which she replied "poor people". It struck me then as it does now,
that my four year old daughter did not acknowledge she was visiting
her great grandmother, but she did recognise poverty. Yet, in Jamaican terms, my grandmother was not that poor at all. This focused my
mind on what the stark realities were for my parents back then in
those times when they decided to leave the island

BLACK BRITISH BORN

Since the fifties and sixties, we have seen the living standards in the
United Kingdom improve dramatically, but this has not been mir-
rored in the Third World. I can, therefore, understand and see why
Jamaicans now would want to leave Jamaica in search of a better life.
The question is; "What way is this better life procured"? This also
raises questions about those of us who were born and brought up
in the United Kingdom: "What have we achieved with our relative
advantage over those wishing to come here in pursuit of better lives,
and: "should we be doing better?" Being born and bred in England,
so to speak, I have a love and a passion for Britain. Although some of
her institutions have problems in terms of diversity, and her weather
is a bit precarious, she still holds a great fascination for me. This is
why I am writing this book, because I want to see Britain thrive as well
as us, as a community, thrive within that context.

POPULATION OF JAMAICA

Outlined below is the general size of the Jamaican population, the spread within the main cities and the racial mix, as it stood in 2002.

People

Population	2,680,029 (2002 estimate)

Largest cities, with population

Kingston	538,100 (1995)
Spanish Town	92,383 (1991)
Montego Bay	83,446 (1991)

Ethnic groups

Black African	91 percent
Mixed	7 percent
East Indian	1 percent
Other	1 percent

There is a Jamaican motto, which says, "Out of Many, One People," suggesting that despite racial and ethnic differences, all groups live united as one Jamaican people.

It is said however, that there are more Jamaicans living outside Jamaica than living in, Jamaica.

JAMAICAN REPUTATION

It is of some concern to me to see that the Jamaican reputation has been so badly tarnished in recent years. Born to Jamaican parents; I take pride in the fact that I am of Jamaican descent. Being the oldest of six children, I saw my parents work hard to provide a better life for us. They toiled in the wet and cold, rarely taking time off let alone holidays. They were, and still are, law-abiding and true to the Jamaican spirit of hard work and discipline. Indeed, this was true of most West Indian families at that time; the community spirit in those days was strong and vibrant. There is a clear distinction between the newly arrived Jamaicans and those who have been here for some time. The Jamaicans that came in the early years were migrant workers coming largely from the out of town areas and the countryside of Jamaica. Jamaica in those days was a calm colonial, territory that had its fair share of poverty. Yet the attitude of the people was friendly, jolly and pleasant, whilst standing firm in the face of adversity. A good indicator of the mood of the people at that time was the music. The lyrical content and mood of music in the early years was smooth and often about relationships, love and the general struggle for a better life.

Harry Bellefonte's hit record "Oh island in the sun" illustrated that mood. The late great Robert Nester Marley's music often had love as its theme, whilst also touching upon the oppression of ordinary people, with words like *"get up stand up, stand up for your rights"*. Years after Marley's death, the music still strikes a chord, and has clearly stood the test of time. The music then was generally more rhythmic and smooth. Over the years, the mood of Jamaica has changed. The music has become harsher, the lyrics more graphic and explicit; sex has replaced love and the *'bad man'* concept has become the only solution to the struggle of life. The recent imposition of visas on Jamaicans wishing to travel to this country, is another step towards controlling gun violence on our streets. Again, the inference from this policy is that the Government believe the recent influx of Jamaicans has fuelled an already volatile gun crime situation. Other countries have subsequently emulated the United Kingdom by issuing visa restrictions on Jamaicans, some of them are Caribbean countries themselves.

Some of the new arrivals have a different attitude and a different value system. Whether the change in attitude over the years is due to the harsh realities, poverty and deprivation in Jamaica, is debateable. The Jamaican dollar had sunk to over JA$115 to £1 sterling, at the time of writing this book. In economic terms this means that imports to Jamaica, particularly manufactured goods, will be very expensive. The irony of this is that exports from Jamaica should be stimulated as labour cost will be relatively cheap and, therefore, Jamaican produce should be relatively attractive on the world market. The Jamaican national debt weighs heavily on its economy. The World Bank posted on its web site that in 2002 there was 67.5% debt to GDP (gross domestic product) expressed as a ratio. This can be interpreted as, for every JA$1 that is made domestically in Jamaica, 67.5 cents is used to service the debt. Jamaica's prime industry is tourism. Some say this does not come without a price, the erosion of local culture and custom. Others argue that local custom and culture can live side by side with a healthy tourist trade.

INDEPENDENCE

In the 1970s Jamaica was one of the fastest growing economies within the region. What happened since then, to bring Jamaica to its economic apocalypse, is outside the scope of this book and would require a lot more research on my part before I could give an informed view. But the question I must raise is: "Does Great Britain owe Jamaica a duty of care as its previous colonial master and before that, slave master: not to mention the sheer brutality of the slave trade and its aftermath? Or does independence mean Jamaica, and other countries like her, must go it alone and to pitch herself at the mercy of the world market?" The concept of the free market suggests that labour (people) will move to wherever work exists. Jamaicans are the living testimony of this, in that they have moved to all corners of the world, near and far. To unlikely countries, such or Nicaragua and Ethiopia. Some have achieved high office e.g. US Secretary of State Colin Powell is of Jamaican extraction; others have become businessmen/women and professionals.

JAMAICAN ACHIEVERS

The saying *"We likkle but we tallawah"* (small country but big on world impact) can be applied to many aspects of Jamaican life. Listed below are a few famous Jamaicans.

Mary Seacole was born in Jamaica, where she learned nursing skills from her mother who kept a boarding house for invalid soldiers. Mary came to Britain in 1845, where she applied to the War Office offering her services as a nurse to British troops engaged in the Crimean War. However, she was turned down because of colour prejudice. Mary was not discouraged by this and funded her own trip to the Crimea, where she set about nursing the sick and wounded. She also started her own shop, selling herbal medicine.

The Hon. Marcus Garvey ,the great Jamaican orator, after returning from a long tour of the Caribbean and Central America, to the USA in July 1921, had problems obtaining a re-entry visa, yet at that time Garvey was one of the most powerful leaders among the Black masses in the United States.

Robert Nester Marley, the man who brought reggae music to the international stage. Unfortunately he died, tragically, at the age of 36 but his longevity lives on. He was a social activist, a lyrical master and a champion for the poor and disadvantaged. His music leaves an indelible mark on our past, present, and future struggle to secure an harmonious existence.

Bill Morris, (retired General Secretary Transport and General Workers Union) was born in 1938 and educated at Mizpah School in Manchester, Jamaica. In 1954 he joined his widowed mother in the Handsworth District of Birmingham, England. The Transport & General Workers Union is the largest industrial trade union in the UK, with almost one million members.

United States Secretary of State, Colin Powell, 2001 to 2005 is of Jamaican extraction. He rose to prominence through the US military forces. Having served as Head of the Military, he was considered a realistic candidate for the most powerful office in the world, the American Presidency.

Sporting personalities such as Lennox Lewis, (Heavy Weight Boxing champion of the world) and Linford Christie, (athletics 100 metres Olympic and world champion) need no introduction, they were world champions of Jamaican extraction.

The sporting achievement of Jamaica, particularly in athletics, is something to behold, given the size and population of the Country. The Jamaican contribution to popular culture around the world is astounding, even some of the language used on London's streets by youngsters has its roots in Jamaica. The vast majority of Jamaicans are hard working and creative. However, others have joined the criminal fraternity; sadly it is these few that have attracted the most media attention.

CONTRAST WITH OTHER ISLANDS

I have visited Barbados, another West Indian Island. It is a beautiful island. In essence, Barbados has a different kind of beauty to that of Jamaica. The Landscape of Jamaica is irresistible, but the infrastructure of Barbados is equally as irresistible. The economy of Barbados is relatively strong and its tourist industry appears to be booming. The standard of education in Barbados is high, the level of crime is relatively low. The quality of life for the ordinary Barbadian is quite high when measured against third world standards and, in a sense, one can see a society that on face value appear to be at peace with itself. Having said this, I don't know enough about the commerce of Barbados and its economic structure to form a valid and unfettered opinion.

I have heard some people define Barbados as "little England in the West Indies", and I must admit, there are many similarities. To me this is a good thing, because Barbados appears to have emulated the good things that we, in Britain perhaps, take for granted. The judiciary, infrastructure, roads, public transport and healthcare all appear to be a microcosm of Britain.

One interesting point, what I found fascinating in Barbados was that the young people loved the music emanating from Jamaica. This, I understand, is also true of the other West Indian Islands. It struck me then, as it does now, that the Jamaican influence on popular culture is as strong now as it ever was. This is something that Jamaica has in abundance; music has long-since been a worldwide export for Jamaica.

DISCIPLINE LESSONS TO BE LEARNED

The questions we must ask ourselves as a community living in the United Kingdom is, "are there lessons that can be learned from the Caribbean experience, with regard to education and discipline? Can the 'Mother Land' take lessons with regard to education and discipline from countries which it once ruled?" A sobering thought.

Just by way of a final thought on the matter, I urge you to think about this. Our parents or grand parents uprooted themselves from their loved ones and communities within the West Indies and travelled to the United Kingdom. Is it not therefore incumbent upon us to move forward in a manner that will grace the opportunity the first generation have afforded us?

OUT OF MANY ONE PEOPLE

An island and a people born out of slavery.
How they worked, toiled and showed the utmost bravery,
freedom and emancipation was a must,
because in the Lord Almighty we placed our trust.

From Montego Bay, Kingston and Port Royal,
the inhabitants of Jamaica always remain loyal.
Out of many, one people, but, out of one people, many have travelled.
Those that travel the World far and wide,
always remember Jamaica is where we used to reside.

A part of our heritage lies right here in the United Kingdom.
They enslaved us, and ultimately gave us our freedom.
Now we are here, we must play an integral part in the betterment of society,
and we must make this our overarching priority.

We march forward looking for justice, equality and inclusiveness,
we must leave behind shallow thinking, and outright obtrusiveness.
Time to wake up and pay homage to our heritage,
as we continue our ongoing pilgrimage.

Richard Todd

CHAPTER IV

EDUCATION

INTRODUCTION

Education is the cornerstone of any modern society. The Oxford dictionary defines it as; "the systematic instruction, school and training in preparation for life". I have to say, it is singularly the best present a parent can give a child. A philosopher once said; "Give a man fish he eats for a day, but teach him to fish and he can feed himself for life".

SCHOOL IN THE SIXTIES

As you might expect, school in the sixties was difficult for Black children in England. Ignorance and prejudice were always simmering, not only amongst the pupils, as you might expect but the teachers also. When I started school there were only two or three Black children in the whole school, but for all that it was an enjoyable experience. Being a child at the time, one had a natural way of getting on with things. There was an element of name-calling and general bravado from the other children, which I did not take seriously at the time, but in today's society it would have been taken far more seriously.

Some of the teachers had not seen or taught children of colour before and, therefore, they had grave misgivings about our ability long before they even knew us. Some teachers at that time were suffering from what I call, "Post Colonial Syndrome" this being the belief that any non-white from the colonies had less cognitive abilities than the host community.

One teacher, at primary school, never really made eye contact with me in the whole three terms that she taught my class. On one particular occasion she set some work and began walking around the classroom, as teachers often do, looking over the pupils' shoulders, making comments about the work to each child. When she came to me she uttered the words; "Is that the best you can do?" to which I replied; "yes miss". She then walked away. However, when she wrote my school report she included this incident and gave the impression that she had really tried to assist me. In a sense she tried to mislead my parents into believing that I was a poor pupil. As a child, I had an innate sense of when an adult was cold towards me; this teacher was as cold as ice. Fortunately, she only remained at the school for one year, but it was one year too long as far as I was concerned.

PARENTAL INFLUENCE

As a young child I was on my best behaviour in the presence of my parents, or any adult that even remotely knew them. At school it was the same thing, if the teacher uttered the immortal words; "I will tell your parents" the fear and trepidation that ensued was overwhelming, some teachers knew this and used it, surreptitiously, as a disciplinary tool. The fear of being disciplined at school paled into insignificance when compared with discipline at home. I call it; "parental control by proxy". However, even in those times there was evidence that discipline in schools was beginning to deteriorate. My parents made my brothers and sisters and me acutely aware even as children, of the need for and importance of education from an early age. As a young man I felt that I knew best and did not quite grasp the nettle immediately, as was probably the case for many young men at that time. I joined in with the self-indulgence of the so-called "raving culture" as a teenager. This was a culture of music, dancing, drinking and boy meets girl. This became the order of the day and little else mattered. Despite the protestations of my parents, in particular my father, I was going down a road from which, had I continued I would have had little chance of return. Looking back at that period I realise how obtuse and shallow incessant partying was, it acted as a form of escapism from the realities of life. It was the point where Black teenagers were joining in the concept of teenage culture which was seen as an alien concept to the black parents who felt helpless to understand or control it. Some people adopted it as a lifestyle and continued at the same tempo well into adulthood, resulting in a lifetime of escapism. A 'career raver' renders themselves almost redundant in terms of the wider community struggle for a better life.

LOW EXPECTATIONS

It was in these early years that I was to experience both overt and covert racism in various forms but, in a strange yet poetic sense, it coloured my life forever. With the benefit of hindsight, my first negative encounters with institutions began at school, although at the time I did not know it. At the ripe old age of fifteen, my mother and I had a meeting with the school's Careers Officer, who advised me that I should take up an unskilled job in a local telecommunications factory. There was no mention of any professions nor was there any mention of a trade. I believe this low level of expectation to be a macrocosm of what was happening to Black youth at that time. Whether the Careers Officer was merely reflecting the sentiment of the school, or whether it was his own interpretation of my ability is unclear.

Another point in principle affected my younger sister as she was about to embark upon her "O" (ordinary) levels. At the time my sister had a good White school friend with whom she studied and played; in fact she used to assist the other child with her homework. "O" (ordinary) levels were higher grade of qualification than CSEs and generally acted as the route to "A" (advance) levels. When it came to the time to select which pupils would sit "O" (ordinary) levels or CSEs, my sister was relegated to sitting for CSEs, and the White child was selected for "O" (ordinary) levels. This happened after my sister had been told she would be doing "O" (ordinary) levels. My mother took great exception to this and arranged to meet the Headmaster. When the Headmaster was asked why my sister was relegated to sitting CSEs, he had no definitive answer. My mother pointed out that my sister always helped the other child with her homework, to which he replied; "Who is the other child"? At that point my mother said that it was not for her to tell him how to discharge his responsibilities. I will not go into all the detail but, what I will say is this, if time is the master then let the master speak. My sister is now a Director within a major charitable organisation, whereas her friend has a nondescript career. What is clear, is that the limited expectation which the educational system had of us has been unequivocally superseded.

OUR CHILDREN TODAY

Children seldom see the correlation between a good education and the quality of later life, sometimes referred to as 'deferred gratification'. In fact the pressure on children now, to conform to popular culture, is unyielding. Children nowadays know more about designer labelled products than they do about their origins. Worse still, a large element of them have become rowdy, undisciplined and disrespectful. Yet we as Black parents remain collectively silent whilst this is happening. A simple acid test for those of us who disbelieve that our children have become unruly, is to take a bus outside an inner city school just after school finishes. Try it if you dare. Even standing at the bus stop where the children congregate is an experience in itself. Just listen to them, observe their body language and general behaviour, and then decide for yourselves. The shouting, the screaming;

the swearing, the sexual innuendo, almost hedonistic, behaviour is simply quite nauseating. As if that's not bad enough, when they communicate with each other using street slang, it sounds almost primitive. I heard one young boy answering his mobile phone where he simply uttered the following, "yo, whats gwanin, ya ya ya ya, yes blood, laters, laters, laters". **Sasha Baron Cohen** (Ali G), the comedian, would have a field day. He makes a good living by portraying a character who talks like this all the time. These children think it sounds good, but it's actually a joke and the joke is not just on them, its on us as a community. Diction is a key life skill that should be observed in everyday conversation if it is to be perfected. A Leading African American actor, comedian and author, Bill Crosby, was reported to have said, that "Everyone knows its important to speak English, except these knuckleheads, you can't be a doctor with that crap coming out of your mouth". The counter argument raised by others; is that street slang should be encouraged, as it is a badge of identity, without which one will achieve nothing.

Some of our children's behaviour is such that they are not only an embarrassment to themselves, but also to the wider community. The harrowing thing is, they don't know it, or maybe they simply don't care. You could argue that our children are just as ill behaved as their White peers, and that this may be a part of the general decline in standards and values. Even young girls are more violent today than ever before: not only to each other, but also towards boys. But, as my mother used to say, "if you're a fool don't let the world know"; and this is exactly what we are doing, when we effectively bury our head in the sand. This all brings to mind a movie, (Children of The Corn) which I watched years ago. In it, children took over from adults, in fact they ruled and terrorised adults. It was supposed to be a scary fiction movie, but in a strange way it had an element of truism. It is not uncommon, in wider society now to hear of children as young as twelve terrorising the elderly on an estate. The question I would therefore ask is this, "Are children now beginning to frighten us?, are they in the driving seat?" Unlike the movie there is no fanciful conclusion; indeed there is no caped crusader to the rescue. The solution has to come from within the community.

If these children hold our future in their hands, then what future have we got? There is a Jamaican saying which states, "W*e run things, it is not things that run we*". Any society or community where the youngsters do not respect the elders and get away with it, is a community in turmoil. Just think about all the knowledge and experience that is held by the older members of our community, yet the younger generation do not value it. If the youth of today do not listen to the more experienced within our community, they run the risk of repeating the errors of the past. Oddly enough in some cases, a youngster will listen to a popular-peer group member, more so than an adult or a teacher, particularly if that popular-peer group member is loud and domineering. The upshot of this is that a child is perceived to be a 'nerd', because he or she does not wear designer clothes, or because they refuse to use street slang, or generally do not fit the mould of popular culture. Someone who works hard and focuses on their studies may well find themselves being classed as a 'nerd' or 'boffin'. What the peer-group do not realise is that the child labelled as the 'nerd' could one day be their employer, doctor, lawyer or accountant. This popular culture, therefore, is counterproductive, and is stifling education within our community, as well as having a negative impact on society of which we are all a part.

The biggest barrier to learning faced by Black pupils in school is what their friends think of them, according to research by Dr Sewell of Leeds University in 2002. Of the 150 15 year old Black pupils surveyed, 80% said peer pressure was the biggest barrier to their learning. In my view, someone who does not encourage you to achieve your full potential can never be your true friend. Dare I say, they are the enemy within, the wolf in sheep's clothing.

DISCIPLINE

The young have always had a degree of spontaneity and freedom and most parents would not wish to take that away but, when they see their children going too far, it is a parental responsibility to curb their child's behaviour. I am not suggesting that anyone goes out on the street and tackles the first unruly child they see; indeed, that could be counterproductive. Rather, I am suggesting that we need to do two things as parents;

1. Have effective control of our own children; know where they are, what they are doing and, with whom.
2. Empower organisations and government institutions to deal effectively and fairly with unruly children. Such empowerment must include transparency and accountability in order that the community can take some comfort that the aims and objectives are sound and that practices are being carried out competently and objectively.

Some of our children are not mature enough to deal with the level of freedom they currently have. "*The devil makes work for idle hands*". It is a parental responsibility to ensure the good behaviour of one's children and we must never lose sight of this. The Government have recognised this and are now holding parents responsible for their children's truancy from school. But I struggle to understand the Government when on one hand it wants parents to be more responsible for their children's behaviour, and on the other they frown on physical punishment of the child. I got smacked as a child and I thank the lord that I did. I am not an overtly spiritual man, but I do have an honest belief in the essential Christian doctrine of equality and fairness to all. To this end I shall quote two verses from the bible, *Proverbs 13:24:"He that spareth his rod hateth his son: but he that loveth him chasteneth him betimes. Proverbs 23:13-14: "Withhold not discipline from the child, for if you strike and punish him with the rod, he will not die. Thou shalt beat him with the rod, and shalt deliver his soul from hell.* The Oxford dictionary defines discipline as a "branch of instruction, mental and moral training". Discipline is a pre-requisite to education; without it the opportunity to learn is impaired. For any disciplinary measure to work it must have teeth in order to dissuade the child. There is an old Jamaican saying which states, "*if you play with puppy, the puppy will lick your mouth*", (familiarity breeds contempt). This means in practice that if you play with a child too much without clear boundaries, the child will become over-familiar and consequently disrespectful. Another saying is "*bend the tree when it's young, because when it is older one will be unable to easily bend it*". In other words it is easier to discipline a person when they are young, as children are more receptive to new ideas. Discipline begins in the home. This book covers discipline in more detail later, in the chapter entitled "The Family".

A child must learn to be a good citizen, because only by being a good citizen can they benefit from a more cohesive and law-abiding society.

In the final analysis liberty and freedom are for those who can abide by it. Good citizenship is a life-skill.

EXCLUSIONS

The number of young Black boys excluded from school is at an all time high, 2/3 of all school exclusions are Afro-Caribbean boys. Some would argue that the system does not understand them and, therefore, the system is failing them. We as parents should understand our children; after all, at the very least we know where they're coming from, as we had a part to play in that process. Can we put the problems we face as a community solely at the Government's door?

or, are we complicit after the act? We can only begin to deal with issues affecting our community if we are honest with ourselves. Black boys are demonised within the education system. In some cases they are excluded for minor infringements, which perhaps their White peers would not have been excluded for the same misdemeanours. A teacher once said; " the problem with Black boys is that their body grows quicker than their mind, and, as such, they are big in body, but small in mind".

Diane Abbott, Member of Parliament, stated in the Sunday Observer; "there is a silent catastrophe happening in Britain's schools in the way they continue to fail Black school children. When African and Caribbean children enter the school system at five, they do as well as the White and Asian do in tests. By the age of eleven, their achievement levels begin to drop off. By sixteen, there has been a collapse". Diane was to court controversy when she opted to send her son to an independent fee paying school, having previously argued against it. Diane pointed to the poor performance of the Black boys at her local schools as being central to her decision. What Diane has inadvertently done is raise the level of awareness surrounding the under-achievement of Black boys.

A Black US academic and an advisor to President Clinton, Dr Richard Majors, appointed by the government in 2001 to tackle under-achievement by Black boys in North of England schools, stated that Britain faced a national emergency if it failed to tackle the problems of these pupils, who are being marginalized.

CURRENT SITUATION

The current situation regarding Black Caribbean educational achievement is cause for concern. The histogram below highlights the recent position;

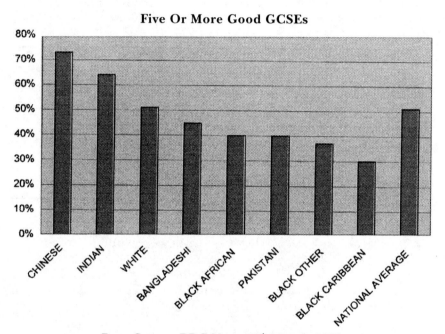

Five Or More Good GCSEs

Data Source BBC News: 4ᵗʰ March 2003

This figure may have altered by the time this book is published, but it is not the specific that concerns us it is the trend that we should concern ourselves with. Our community is 21% below the average and a staggering 43% less than the most academically successful ethnic group the Chinese. On the basis of the above figure we are the lowest educated racial group. If we transpose these results into future employment and quality of employment, we will not be in a position to compete for the better professional jobs and, therefore, our status in society may well remain, at best, limited. Furthermore, it is perhaps worth noting that Black Caribbean girls do a lot better than Black Caribbean boys.

A significant proportion of Black parents have turned their backs on the state education system in favour of the private sector. Other parents move to neighbourhoods where they are in the catchment area for their desired state school. But many parents fall into a trap of having to send their child to the local school, a school which might not be their first choice. In fact for many parents there is no choice, (Hobson's choice). In reality, I would say that choice is for those who can afford it and Hobson's choice is all that is left for those unfortunate enough not to reside in the correct catchment area, or who can not afford it. This is true not only of the Black community but society as a whole. The problem a poor Black family may have, is that when they send their child to certain under-performing schools, they could be inflicting irreparable damage to their child and could lose their child to the streets and even gang culture. Other racial issues compound this further, and the child will be ill equipped to face this throughout life.

There are too many black men who are poorly educated. Of course there will be individuals that buck the trend, but it is the trend that must be dealt with if we, as a community, are to move forward. Too many poorly educated Black men, who are less educated than their parents and, in some cases, grandparents, should be a concern to us as a community. The link between poor education, crime and anti-social behaviour is irrefutable.

Tony Sewell, a Black Leeds University Lecturer and journalist, states; "It's simply youth culture and does not inspire intellectual interest. It is actually to do with propping up a big commercial culture, to do with selling trainers [sneakers], selling magazines, rap music and so on." Tony Sewell goes on to accuse the Black community of being unwilling to confront the detrimental role Black youth culture might play in children's school lives. He goes on to say, "I am also tired of hearing the excuse that Black students are failing because the curriculum is too Euro-centric. Let's get real."

SUCCESS STORY

A Foundation Church girls school, within a South London inner-city borough, showed remarkable results which completely went against the trend. In terms of diversity, 89% of the pupils were described as non-white. Within this group, (89%) there were Black British, Black other West African, Muslims and Hindus, there were even Portuguese and Cubans. The school population was in excess of 700 pupils. It is exactly the type of school that, if one were to be honest, one would not expect to be doing well if the general statistical trends were to be believed. However, the reality was quite different, the school was performing well above average, 59% of its pupils obtained five or more good GCSEs. Consequently the school was over subscribed by five to one. Their Ofsted (Independent Inspectorate) report 2002, reported the following: "This is a very good school. Leadership is excellent and helps teachers and pupils give their best. Pupils achieve very well in response to high expectations and very good teaching. Standards are above average and show consistent improvement. Pupils' personal development is very good and they develop self-esteem, self-discipline and strong community values. The school gives good value for money. The school has no areas of weakness to be raised".

The Head Teacher had been in post five years to the day at the time of the visit. She was indeed very up-beat about the results of her school. Indeed she had good cause to be. The Head Teacher felt that her strategy of inclusion was central to the school development plan, with a focus on learning and a general refusal to accept nothing but the best from her pupils. It is instilled in the girls that they can achieve anything and go anywhere with hard work and endeavour.

The Head Teacher goes to great lengths to suggest that she is not a social worker in that she is not at the school to solve the children's social problems. Having said this, if social problems act as a barrier to learning, then the Head's objective will be to try and remove that barrier. The school attempts to understand and recognise the needs and wants of the parents with regards to their children, some of the mothers may have had bad experiences with the school in the past and, as a result, there may well be some mistrust. But the school tries to build trust with the parents as part of its core strategy.

The Head Teacher outlined what she would expect of parents in order to assist their children:

1. Understanding skills to help the child.
2. Adjustment in lifestyle; regular sleep, etc.
3. Reduction of negative influences, no video or television in the bedroom.
4. Monitoring phone calls.

The school operates a zero-tolerance disciplinary code that the Head Teacher calls having the girls "under manners"; even girls sucking their teeth can result in some disciplinary action being taken. The Head Teacher also warns her pupils against relationships with boys and points out the pitfalls of such relationships.

The school pursues a fully inclusive curriculum, which celebrates cultural diversity. This in essence teaches the girls to value and respect the culture of others. Children are taught to recognise that all of them are equal in the eyes of God, in line with the Christian ethos. The Christian ethos adopted by the school is not oppressive in that the school does not try to convert children of other faiths, rather what the school does, is recognise spirituality and embraces all faiths. To this end, all children within the school attend and take part in assembly irrespective of religious background, which is in line with the Head Teacher's ethos, that different cultures add to and enrich the learning experience.

The Head Teacher spoke of initial difficulties when she was first appointed and the so-called 'White flight syndrome'. This is where White pupils are moved by their parents to other schools. However her target for the future is for 75% of pupils to obtain GCSE's A to C, in the next 2 years, and it would appear that she is set to achieve this.

BLACK GIRLS CONSISTENTLY OUTPERFORM BLACK BOYS

The fact that Black girls consistently outperform Black boys educationally can create an imbalance in the aspirations between the sexes. If this imbalance were to continue into later life, we could see Black women in higher profile positions compared with their Black male counterparts. This could then lead to a lack of eligible Black men as partners for these educated women. Black men have pride and dignity, and the idea of not being the breadwinner is alien and extremely challenging to them in the context of a relationship. Consequently, the women could begin to consider taking a partner from another community. Yet the real danger for society lays in the fact that the men could cause civil unrest if they are not afforded opportunity. Education may not necessarily be the panacea to social deprivation, but it goes a long way towards reducing the worst symptoms.

DISRUPTIVE PUPILS

Schools have been given greater powers to permanently exclude violent and disruptive pupils under new laws. Targets to cut the number of exclusions will be scrapped and parents will be legally forced to control their children's behaviour. Panels hearing appeals against exclusions will, for the first time, be empowered to consider the effect of a child's behaviour on the school. Schools and local authorities will also face greater pressure to ensure that children who have been excluded from one school are taken on at another. The Government, at the time of drafting this book, announced plans to extend court-imposed parenting orders, forcing parents to take responsibility for their child's behaviour and stop them being disruptive. Strategies will also be devised for dealing with parents who are themselves violent or abusive towards school staff. The new measures are to be backed with more cash for in-school units which place badly disruptive pupils back on track. Alongside the measures will be mandatory admissions forums to ensure that excluded children are brought back into education. There will be "swift action" against local education authorities that fall behind in providing full-time education to all permanently excluded youngsters.

These plans are said to put some parents under pressure to ensure they take control of their children with regards to discipline and control, but this conjures up more discussion as we know that the vast majority of parents have the best interest of their children at heart and do instil adequate levels of discipline, However, for those who have children in schools where reputations are not too healthy, they have more chance of being 'caught up', labelled and excluded. Before now there were more safeguards in place which made the process to exclude children longer, but now if more children are being excluded and new schools are not found quickly enough to make youngsters feel a part of the system, then the streets will become an increasingly intense powder keg. Any new programme that the Government intends to put together will need to effectively promote good behaviour. This is not only about putting into place constraints for children, it is about helping them take control; of their feelings, emotions and interactive skills, it also means working closer with parents. There is a requirement for enhanced teacher training, enabling advanced communication techniques to be taught, better working between health and education to spot and tackle problems and more support for young children at the start of school.

One final thought for you to consider is this, education is the passport to the World and all its glories. A Head Teacher once described education as; "the gateway to the world," a sentiment that I echo. It follows, therefore, that a lack of education restricts freedom and limits opportunity. We, as individuals and as community, must crave knowledge in the same way we crave good food.

EDUCATION IS FOR LIFE

Education is our right,
inertia and apathy is our plight.
Even with designer clothing, nightlife and a fast car,
without education it won't take you far.

Knowledge skills and discipline,
I know this has a familiar ring.
Lets see how far you can go without education.
It may not be the panacea to social deprivation,
but it is the only way to obtain true emancipation.

Why go out and buy your child expensive gear,
When in their mind there is limited education and knowledge there?
Education has longevity,
materialism has a certain depravity.

The best present a parent can give,
is the education that will stay with them as long as they live.

Richard Todd

MAN'S BASIC NEED TO SUCCEED

A hungry man does not give a damn.
All he cares about is the next plate of food.
That's not rude, that's not even crude,
it's just his hungry mood.

A hungry man does not care about ideology,
for this he need make no apology.
'Maslow' the great management scholar, once said
"Man must tend to his immediate need,"
it is not greed; it is merely what he needs to succeed.
There can be no long term,
if he cannot survive the short term.

Now he has moved forward in his evolution,
what is his resolution?
Is merely a plate of food enough,
or is he made of sterner stuff?

For him to merely stand still,
means he does not fit the bill.
He has to instil the will to fulfil.
He has to posses the will.
He has to posses the skill.
The will must exceed the skill.
He must stick to it like a military drill.

To stand still over the long term, is to regress.
This is something he has to address.
Failing this he will end up in an absolute mess,
without anywhere to go and without redress.

He must hunger for knowledge,
in the same way he once hungered for food,
to do so would indeed be cunning and shrewd.
After all, knowledge is power,
and if he is to bloom like a budding flower,
he must taste whether it is bitter, sweet or sour.

Richard Todd

CHAPTER V

LOCAL GOVERNMENT & EMPLOYMENT PHILOSOPHY

INTRODUCTION

The employment situation is cause for some concern. The hopes and dreams that education and better qualifications would hold the key to overcoming job disadvantage among young Black men have been discouraging. If Black boys are underachieving at school; then it follows that they will struggle with regard to employment. We have to accept that unemployment is irrefutably linked to quality of education. But what of the qualified Black man are his job prospects any better? The truth of the matter is this; the Black man will still struggle regardless of qualification. This is indeed a fact of employment life.

EMPLOYMENT

David Blackaby, an expert on the labour market at the University of Swansea, says legislation designed to combat racial discrimination has failed. In the 30 years since the Race Relations Act was passed; the position of Black people in the labour market appears to have got worse.

We as the Black community must acknowledge that we are disadvantaged in the employment market, it is only by acknowledging this as our reality that we can begin to do something about it. One of the hardest situations to acknowledge is the law of comparative advantage (job market favours some at the expense of other workers), but acknowledge it we must if we are to move on. When I say "acknowledge it", I do not mean that we just walk away and leave it; no, quite the contrary. Where there is inequality we should highlight it, and try and change the mindset of that particular organisation or institution. What I am saying, however, is that we must get real when it comes to employment opportunity and base our employment or career strategies on this premise.

Globalisation and the expansion of the European Common Market could both impact upon future job opportunities. Globalisation could mean jobs being moved to different parts of the world, whereas the expansion of the European Common Market could mean an in-flow of migrant labour to this country. The new wave of migrants will no longer come from the ex-colonies but, to a larger extent, they will come from Eastern Europe. The movement of jobs from the UK to other parts of the world by multinational companies will also have an impact on the home job market. This all leads to one conclusion; the job market in future will become ever more competitive. A more competitive job market will mean trouble ahead for the working class, and for the Black community, who form a substantial part of this group and who already struggle in the current employment climate. The question is this, "Could globalisation and the expansion of the European Common Market expand the ever-growing underclass in the United Kingdom?"

REJECTION

On countless occasions in the 1980s and 1990s I have phoned a pro-spective employer in response to an advert and over the phone, I have given a synopsis of my experience and qualifications. At this stage the employer still has no inclination of my ethnicity and proceeds to provide lavish details about the position, in some cases asking about my availability to start, then arranging an interview. Can you imag-ine the shock and horror when the prospective employer sees me? If there are others in the waiting room the employer will invariably go to them first, thinking that they are the applicant. The interviewer's opening gambit is; "just to let you know, Mr Todd, we have had a huge response to the advertisement" When the prospective employer plays this particular chess move, I don't wait for checkmate; I already know my fate. Some of you will instinctively know what I am talking about, others will say maybe my analysis; or take on the situation, was wrong. But my answer to this is, "It did not happen to me once, or even twice, it happened too many times to mention". At one point I even thought about saying to the prospective employer "By the way I am Black," as a way of saving time, but after serious consideration I felt that it might have been counterproductive to do so. My only regret is that I did not record each occasion.

One thing that concerns me is the way management can, wittingly or unwittingly, use Black staff in a surreptitious way. I recall one par-ticular occasion where I was asked to undertake an audit of a Black organisation, with immediate effect. Management had some con-cerns about the way this organisation was being run and this was on-going for years. I was pulled off another audit to conduct the audit of this organisation. Management felt that by using me, a Black auditor, they could not be accused of being racist. I was to find myself always undertaking audits with an element of controversy or ethnic issues. I found this a difficult and humbling experience, but in another sense it made me become a better professional. All I ever wanted was to do a good, professional, job, free from encumbrance.

Black managers sometimes experience difficulties with members of staff who do not readily accept their authority. Very often the leap-frog approach is used. This is where a junior member of staff will deliberately report to another manager, one rank higher than that of the Black manager. In other cases, staff will challenge the authority the Black manager in a more direct way. A Black manager will continually have to prove themselves. You may argue that this is no different to the white manager. It is my experience that the main difference is the time taken to win the confidence of other managers and staff. A Black manager will have to work longer and harder to achieve the same level of respect as his or her White counterpart.

We must begin to control our mindset in order to cope with the additional pressure that racial disadvantage will pose throughout our lives. Our attitude to a job of work cannot be the same as our White counterparts. Our White counterparts are three times more likely than us, the Black community, to obtain new positions in other organisations. This is an irrefutable fact of life. We should pursue what I call; a consolidation strategy when working for any organisation. The essence of consolidation is the retention of wealth or earnings. The concept of saving for a rainy day is our reality. Any axe that may fall within an organisation may well fall on our heads and we know particularly as Black men, that this means continued insecurity. Outsourcing, contracting out, externalising, downsizing; all have the same meaning for the Black workforce, redundancy and insecurity is the order of the day.

If we emulate other communities, in terms of the way we consume and spend our money, we will struggle perpetually to move away from being a wage slave. We have a meagre slice of the economic cake and, therefore, we must eat it sparingly, if it is to last. When we hold any position, we have to treat it with due reverence, as we know that it is precious to us and, if lost, we could be a long time unemployed; no matter what qualifications we may hold. I refer to this as; "the consolidation strategy", which dictates that one holds on dearly to what one has and builds upon it in a structured way.

Sometimes I marvel at the way some workers treat their jobs with a level of impunity. Often openly disrespecting the job. It is not a luxury we can afford. A job, to us, is something to behold, protect and respect, because we know in our hearts and minds that it is a very limited resource and with any limited resource you protect and utilise it. What we have we desperately try to hold on to. Social, or upward mobility, is a lot harder for us as a community; than the host community, it is a fact of life that we must acknowledge. We must smell the coffee and wake up, anything else would be a dream. Remember dreams are for those who sleep and life is for us to keep.

OVERT DISCRIMINATION

My first definitive adult encounter with an overtly racist organisation was back in the mid 1970s. A tabloid newspaper was running an advertisement for trainee computer operators for a training organisation, and guaranteed placements after training. To apply for this, one had to sit a test. I applied, therefore, and duly sat the test. I remember on the day of the test that there were hundreds of people there. Having sat the test, we were allowed a short break to wait for the results. We were then called back we took our seats and waited for the results. Fortunately my name was called out in due course and as a result I was invited to attend an interview a few days later. Full of youthful enthusiasm I attended the interview, only to be told by the interviewer that, unfortunately, she would not be able to offer me a position as a trainee as it would be difficult to place me at the end of the course, since prospective employers were unlikely to want a Black person. So they could not risk training me, if it was going to be difficult to place me. Needless to say I felt deflated and very angry, it was a cold and crude experience. The matter-of-fact tone with which the interviewer conveyed the message, left me distraught. Whether the training organisation concerned was reflecting the needs and wants of its clients, or whether they took it upon themselves as a policy I will never know, perhaps it no longer matters. However, time was to prove the best healer, and you know they say the lord works in mysterious ways, and this I was about to find out would ring true in my life. The subsequent training that I acquired in accountancy and internal audit, I may never have acquired if I had been accepted on the computer operator-training course.

CUT PUBLIC SECTOR EXPENDITURE

When West Indians first arrived in this Country, they were employed, to a large extent, in the Public Sector which included the Health Service, public transport and Local Government. At the forefront of government macro economic policy in the early eighties was controlling public sector expenditure. The Conservative Government of the day sought to reduce public sector expenditure and by doing so reduce inflation and the level of direct taxation. The rationale being, that by reducing the money supply to the economy, inflationary pressures would be curtailed. Hospitals were closing down the length and breadth of the country. Downsizing, streamlining, outsourcing and contracting out services became the norm in the public sector. Workers were no longer comfortable in their jobs, as no sooner one reorganisation was complete, another began and each reorganisation could mean unemployment. In many of these institutions, the concept of 'jobs for life' was to disappear forever.

LOCAL DEMOCRACY

The Race Relations Act 1976, as amended by the Race Relations (Amendment) Act 2000, makes it unlawful to discriminate against anyone on grounds of race, colour, nationality (including citizenship), or ethnic or national origin. The amended Act also imposes general duties on many public authorities to promote racial equality, and also to monitor and publish the results.

In our day-to-day lives we are more likely to seek the services of our Local Authorities than those of Central, Government, yet we possess such limited knowledge about the way Local Government operates. Local Government exists to provide services such as local amenities, housing, town planning, education, social and other support services. We have the right to periodically vote for Councillors in order to influence the way the authority is run. Some of us rarely exercise that right. However, we as a community need to be cognisant with Local Authority practices and procedures; we should never lose sight of the fact that they are there to serve the community, of which we are an integral part.

Local Government in the 1980s began to implement Equal Opportunity Policies (EOP). The underlined themes of these policies were to employ more ethnic minorities and women over time. Some authorities were accused of pursuing EOP policies at the detriment of service delivery. The perception being that services were being compromised by EOP. In my opinion, a good EOP approach is one that appoints the best person for the position irrespective of colour, race, sex, sexual orientation and disability. It is important to note here that EOP does not mean positive discrimination in favour of any one group. In fact, prior to EOP there was a culture of nepotism (who you know), which was widespread within Local Authorities. However, I can see why a society riddled by class structure might struggle with such a basic concept as equal opportunity for all. Our problem as a community is access to training and education in order that we can compete effectively for positions. It would be fair to say that many of the inequalities have its roots firmly planted in the educational system.

I joined Local Government in 1977, before EOP was even a glint in the eye of left-wing politicians. I was appointed as a clerical assistant, the lowest administrative grade. Moving from a clerical assistant grade to a clerical officer grade was the most difficult move I have ever had to make in my working career. This job tested my resolve and my temperament, not that it was difficult; rather there was strict time pressure, as it was a weekly wage payment section. I remember one occasion when the manager asked me to do something unnecessarily complicated. So I suggested that maybe we could approach the matter in another, streamlined, way. The supervisor took one look at me and shouted, "You're paid to do as I say, so just do it". The way he shouted at me was humiliating, which with the benefit of hindsight, showed his insecurity rather than my incredulity. I nearly lost my temper that day, but a colleague of mine who witnessed the incident said "Richard do not compromise yourself by responding, just do what he says". From that day on I knew that I had to develop myself both academically and professionally. It was to mark the starting point of my determination that better must come. I made countless applications within and outside the department. I saw other individuals with less experience appointed over me. I have attended interviews for jobs where the interviewer did not even make eye contact, and I knew within five minutes of the start of the interview that I was wasting my time.

I did finally get a senior clerical position outside the department and this, in a strange way, launched my professional career and ultimately my business career. It was a point from which I have never looked back. This position, nevertheless, had its problems. After successfully doing the job for some time, my line manager asked me if I wanted to go on and set up costing systems on a major recreation centre complex which was just being built. I duly obliged. I saw it as an opportunity to show what I could do, as I would be working on my own and providing building management with up to date costing information on site. Over time, management felt that the position on site had become more high profile, and therefore the job was to be re-graded upwards. My line manager then told me, under the organisation's Equal Opportunities Policy that I would have to apply for what was effectively my job. I duly obliged and applied. You can probably guess what happened, I did not get the job; a young

White female was appointed. She did not really have the experience or qualification to oust me from the job, yet oust me she did. To add insult to injury, I was asked to teach her the job, at which point I thought enough was enough. I told my line manager I was unwilling to train the new appointee, as I was told to. He ordered me to report to Head Office and then told to resume the job I was doing prior to the position in question. I was still not happy and so I sought an audience with the Director. The Director said "Richard, I can see you have been hard done by, leave it with me". Within two months I was offered a similarly graded post which I accepted; but I was clearly a marked man with regard to my line manager. Not too long after that I took a sideways move, to another department at the same grade, to escape the gaze and glare of a line manager waiting to pounce. The young lady who ousted me from my position, not only struggled with the job, but she subsequently got married to one of the departmental managers. The irony of it all was that she was a nice person who got caught up in a situation outside her control. She left the post shortly afterwards. To this day I don't know whether that was racism, nepotism or both.

In those days, generally, White managers found it difficult to recognise quality in a Black person; they could not see past the fact that the person was Black, even today this is still true in some sectors. I would go as far as to say that some White managers feel almost intimidated by the very presence of the Black man, this is often coupled with a certain mistrust.

Whenever I begin a new job, no matter where, I am treated with suspicion on two distinct levels;

1. Can I be trusted?
2. Am I competent?

This you might say is true of any new employee, but what I find to be the real difference between my White counterpart and myself, is the longer length of time taken for me to win the trust of my White colleagues. I usually always found myself having to continually prove myself. Even after being in an organisation for some time, a simple action like talking quietly to another Black person is often viewed with suspicion, and the conspiracy theorists have a field day, it is almost *persona non grata*. Sometimes my White colleagues would ask me "where do you know him/her from, what do they do and what grade are they on". Yet when white people chat, in the corridors and toilets etc, no one gives it a second thought. Having said this, once people begin to know me and find that I am quite approachable and responsive, there is a marked change in attitude. This is the point at which the barrier of skin colour is removed, and the content of character is truly observed.

On one occasion during an interview, the interviewer said openly that he was taking a chance employing me and he asked me graciously not to let him down; he also instructed another senior member of staff to keep an eye on me.

As younger members of staff, some of whom would have attended school with Black children, are now replacing the older ones, there has been a marked improvement in attitude. I am thus optimistic for the future.

In the seventies there was little precedent of Black people doing anything other than manual jobs. So those of us who were looking for a professional career had few role models and mentors. This was coupled with low expectations from employers and the spectre of racial disadvantage. However, it is not until one looks back that one is able to really decipher what was happening. Perhaps this is just as well that I did not understand what was happening at the time, it may have been the Lord's way of preserving my sanity; after all, they say the Lord works in mysterious ways.

COMPULSORY COMPETITIVE TENDERING

In the 1990s the Government of the day introduced Compulsory Competitive Tendering, (CCT). This is where the Private Sector (contractor) tenders for Local Government services, if they can discharge such services at a lower cost base. It became a feeding frenzy for the hungry, private sector, contractors as they fought for the spoils of Local Government and National Health Service (NHS) contracts. CCT was to prove devastating for poorly paid Local Government workers, which included a large Black workforce. The Government of the day failed to provide a quota system to safeguard jobs in the private sector, even though the private sector had no history of equal opportunities. They did however provide a stipulation within the legislative framework that placed a responsibility upon the contractor to continue the employment of staff on the same terms and conditions for a specified period. In essence, the Conservative Government effectively abandoned EOP and in an indirect way blamed it, in part, for the failure of certain Local Authorities. This I could never understand, as even a first year business studies student will know that it is management who are primarily responsible for policy failings and, up until that point there were very few senior Black managers in Local Government. Whether EOP was implemented in a strategic way or whether it was thrust upon an unwitting public sector, is debatable. What is clear, however, is that it was not managed effectively. It is my view that at that time it never had Central Government backing. In other words, it was not cognisant with Central Government policies at the time, and as such was doomed to failure.

The Greater London Authority (GLA) stated that non-white Londoners are between two or three times more likely to be unemployed than their White colleagues. This shows that an enormous job remains to be done in London to eliminate discrimination in the labour market and all other areas of society. Suffice to say that Black men, in particular, have been severely disadvantaged by the high level of outsourcing, downsizing and restructuring, as they find it difficult to find subsequent employment.

CCT had an in-built weakness, in that it did not readily cater for quality and in some cases, effective internal control. In practice, it had the effect of driving down quality and standards, whilst frustrating accountability. We are now seeing some organisations revert to an in-house service. In the finance field, internal audit and accounting services were outsourced in the main to accountancy firms or their satellite companies, which had been set up in order to compete in that market. In essence, profits were being directed towards accountancy firms some of whom had thinly disguised interests in the public sector organisations they served. Internal Audit services have been outsourced in many public sector organisations. Internal audit is the body for reviewing internal control within an organisation. Their role is to review the adequacy and effectiveness of controls within the organisation; to my mind they are an integral part of the governance function within an organisation, to outsource an internal audit department is a contradiction in terms. To externalise an internal audit function serves to weaken that function as a management tool. The practical aspects of outsourcing, is that job opportunities are taken away from the local communities in which they serve, and pass those opportunities to others who bear no allegiance to the communities they serve.

Terms and conditions of employment were effectively eroded as private firms won more and more Local Government contracts. Similar outsourcing was happening throughout the public sector, with the same consequences for Black staff. CCT as a concept proved too difficult for the trade unions to deal with, it was a corporate industrial relations nightmare.

Some Local Authorities used isometric testing of all staff as a means of identifying who would be selected for redundancy or regrading. It was no longer a case of how good one was at one's job;

rather it became how good one was at sitting isometric tests. So, staff that had been employed in their posts for years, found themselves in the position of having to sit tests and compete for their own jobs. This proved to be a crude and expensive way of assessing staff who already worked within the organisation. Surely the real acid test is this, "Is the member of staff in question doing the job of work to a satisfactory standard and quality?" If management do not know this, then perhaps it is they that should sit the isometric test. The real problem that many staff had with the tests was the lack of transparency and accountability, as managers were involved in marking the papers. Many staff saw it as a way management could settle old scores. As a result, many staff that were dissatisfied with the arrangements took their respective employers to Employment Tribunal. It is my view that some organisations factored this into the human resource strategy and in a way expected staff to go to Employment Tribunal.

LOCAL GOVERNMENT FISCAL POLICY

Government policy in the late 1980s was to control public expenditure, Local Government and the National Health Service at the forefront of that policy. The Community Charge (poll tax) was the vanguard of the Local Government fiscal policy. Community Charge was designed to tax all adults over the age of 18 for the local services they received. The underlined Conservative party theory being, that if all individuals were made acutely aware of the cost of providing local services, they would be more likely to vote for a low spending Authority, or at the very least, put pressure on the Authority to reduce costs. In reducing the cost of service provision, the Community Charge payer's liability would consequently be reduced.

Community Charge was a regressive taxation and was unrelated to the ability of the taxpayer to pay. As a regressive form of taxation it impacted upon those in lower or fixed income severely. Just by way of example, to illustrate the point, consider the following;

Taxpayer	Salary p.a.	Tax paid	%of Income
A	£10,000	£1,000	10
B	£100,000	£1,000	1

The illustration clearly shows that tax payers 'A' and 'B' are paying the same tax, £1000. 'A' the poorer of the two, is paying a higher percentage (10%) of his income for Community Charge. On the other hand taxpayer 'B' pays only is 1% of his income, hence the regressive nature of the taxation. As the Black workforce fell in the lower status we, as a community , were particularly adversely, affected. Community Charge failed and was one of the biggest disasters in taxation history in this country.

Council Tax replaced Community Charge. I will not go into details of the merits of one taxation system over and above another as that falls outside the parameters of this book. What worries me, however, is that in recent times we have seen a huge rise, in the level of Council Tax, this is after CCT, outsourcing, externalisation, and ongoing reorganisation. One final mute point on this matter; "With all the Queen's horses and all the Queen's men they can not bring Council Tax down again", so my message to the Government is; "Why all this pain and where is the gain?"

DIVERSITY

Local Authorities have a vital role to play in working towards a more inclusive society. Under the amended Race Relations Act, they have a duty to promote race equality in all their functions: from policymaking and employment, to service provision and procurement.

The new buzz word that has replaced EOP is 'Diversity'. The Audit Commission recently conducted a review on the essence of Diversity and what they have come up with is, in my opinion, not necessarily conclusive but is an indicator to where diversity is going within the public sector. Outlined below are four points they raised from the review;

1. **The Diversity agenda is not about treating everybody in the same way;**
2. **There is a strong business case for Diversity;**
3. **There is a need for shared definitions of the Diversity vision; and;**
4. **Action on Diversity needs to be managed effectively.**

POLITICAL CORRECTNESS

It is now quite common for radio talk show hosts and other media pundits to regularly decry the folly of political correctness. I call it; "the backlash to political correctness", where one takes a few outrageous examples and uses them to belittle the whole concept of Political Correctness. I must admit some of the issues surrounding some areas of political correctness do appear trivial. Inherent in this is, a danger that we can lose sight of the original causes that gave rise to political correctness, some of which have been delineated in my personal experiences as outlined throughout this book. Trivialisation can undermine Political Correctness and this should be guarded against. But those objective commentators who seek to belittle Political Correctness remember this proverb; "before one criticises another, one should walk a mile in that person's shoes". There is a saying, "*He who feels it knows it*". I would like to think that gone are the days when one had to be wary of visiting the local pub at lunch time, in case ones workmates started making jokes about one Black issue or the other. It is amazing how a couple of pints of beer can loosen the tongue. But the moral dilemma I faced was, "do I make a stand or do I cringe in the corner hoping for it to pass. If I make a stand I am considered not to be a team player, if I don't make a stand I am not true to myself."

I WANT MY LIBERTY

In this urban jungle, I call home, created by mankind,
where can I find some peace of mind,
before I leave this world behind?
Or is this a part of the Almighty test,
and do I have to fulfil the rest?

Oh my lord, everyday I do my best.
I try, I contest, anything less would not be in my interest.
However, the reins of economic control,
have caught me in an uncompromising strangle hold.

I want to be free.
I want my liberty.
That is all I plea from thee.
Nonetheless, over the years, I have become weary,
of a world, that has become so much more scary.

Take away my soul,
and you leave me with a heart that is cold.
You take away my pride,
in this wicked world where I reside.
But when you take my self-esteem,
you take away my inner most dream.

Every one has a right to be free,
no matter who they are, or where they are in the economic tree.
Before you stand in judgement,
from your position of relative contentment,
and before you be decry the folly of political correctness,
why not apply the basic acid test.
Walk a mile in my shoe,
and then, see what you would do.

Richard Todd

THE WAY FORWARD

My negative experiences of the Police, Government and private sector institutions inadvertently gave me the extra drive to work harder to achieve my goals. If we succumb to negative opinions by others about us, we will give credence to their perception of us. The reason I have gone to great lengths to tell you this is because I want to strike a chord with you with regard to our past.

We are now in a different situation as a community and we need to move on, we must not forget the negativity of the past, but we must put it to one side in order to move forward and address the problems that confront us in our struggle.

To paint a picture of total negativity would be wrong, there have been a lot of positive experiences also. One thing I will always thank Local Government for, is helping me to develop, professionally and academically, at a time when the private sector would not even have employed me let alone give me a chance to develop. It is that realisation of opportunity that is the focal point of my success today. From leaving a comprehensive school at sixteen, with no particular qualifications to where I am today, 30 years on, is testimony to what can be achieved with hard work and commitment. I have been between a rock and a hard place, I know what it feels like to be starved of opportunity, where hope dwindles. It is an isolated and lonely place, it feels as though you're heading towards the abyss. As a youth, one does not think about time as being a precious commodity. Alas! Time is the most precious commodity in the world, as "it waits for no man". If one does not utilise time in order to develop and mature, it will simply pass you by, and leaving you bitter and unfulfilled. Youth is a gift from the almighty, use it do not abuse it. I say this so that those reading this book do not think that I am speaking from an ivory tower, without empirical knowledge or experience. My experiences as stated in this book, are not unique, but these do represent one story amongst many, highlighting the road we must travel. We must remember, whether we like it or not, we are coming from a long way down society's pecking order. The race however is not for the swift, but who can endure it. Empirical knowledge is the master of all knowledge, if one does not learn from one's own experiences, then who is one going to learn from.

HOW LUCKY YOU ARE

You cannot know how lucky you are,
if you don't look very far.
Young one you must look far and wide,
before you even begin to decide.

Look to countries over yonder,
you will see poverty and deprivation untold,
if you're like me you will begin to wonder,
the fear of abject poverty is something to behold.
Don't be left out in the cold,
do something about it before you're too old.

Remember, youth is a gift of the Almighty,
forget the pursuance of materials as it can become somewhat unsightly.
Think less about me, myself and I,
rather think about our community and things that you might want to try.
Think about the struggle of those that came before you.
In so doing, it will guide you as to what will carry you through.

You cannot taste the sweetness of success,
if you are unable to contest.
It is the world market place that is the acid test.
It indelibly rewards those that deliver upon its request.

There is no substitute for hard work and endeavour.
No matter who you are and how clever.
For anything you want in life you must work hard for it.
No one has a god given right to it,
however success favours those who focus and prepare for it.

You may think this really funny,
but remember not to always measure success in money.
Success can be about self-determination.
It can be about self-preservation.
It can be about career construction.
Or even merely avoiding self-destruction.

What ever is your success measure,
be sure to take from it absolute pleasure.
The fact that you have achieved your personal goal,
is a beauty in life to behold.

Even if you don't achieved your goal,
my word, you will have improved your life, heart and soul.

Richard Todd

CHAPTER VI

CRIME

CRIME OVERVIEW

Gun crime is merely the tip of the iceberg within our community. There are other crimes which form part of the hierarchy of crime in relation to their seriousness. Detailed below is a block chart showing the crime ladder:

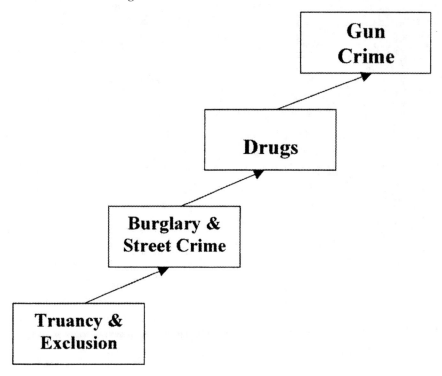

The potential criminal will start as a child from the bottom, truancy & exclusion and could graduate to gun crime. This is an overly simplistic analogy; but for the purpose of fostering strategic thinking, it serves an effective template.

Black people, in particular men, are over represented within the penal system; this is indeed a worry in itself. Somewhere along the so-called hierarchy of crime as outlined in the block chart above, some within the community have lost their way and have fallen foul of the law.

Gun Crime

INTRODUCTION

We have witnessed, in recent years, an alarming increase in crimes involving firearms, the nightmare scenario. To visit any Black nightclub now without being searched meticulously is almost impossible. The intensity of the search is akin to a military checkpoint. One dance flyer I saw recently described its security as 'coalition style', this in itself was deemed to be a selling point. The unspoken fear is always simmering under the surface. The thought that keeps revolving around in my mind is this; "Are we doing this to ourselves?" If this was an institution or others doing this to us we would be furious and demanding change, why then are we not exhibiting the same level of outrage with regard to crime within the Black community? Much of the Black on Black crime as far as the mass media is concerned, is not even newsworthy, and as such is only reported in any detail within the local press and ethnic media.

POLICE RESPONSE TO GUN CRIME

The Police Department responsible for gun crime within the Black Community within London (Operation Trident) have been fighting a battle as the streets become ever more menacing. A quarter of murders in the UK are in London, and 7 out of 10 of those involve Black victims.

Operation Trident is a special Met Police initiative to tackle gun crime amongst London's Black Communities. It has a particular focus on drug-related shootings. The significance of Operation Trident is demonstrated by the fact that it exists as a dedicated Trident Operational Command Unit (OCU) within the Metropolitan Serious Crime Group. Operation Trident has 199 officers, 38 civilian staff and an annual budget of more than £9m, according to information published by the Metropolitan Police.

As of January 2002 the following results had been achieved.

1.   200 suspects arrested and charged.

2. 130 guns seized.
3. 500 kilos of class A drugs seized.

Further information provided by 'Operation Trident' showed the following level of offending:

TRIDENT LEVEL OF OFFENDING FINANCIAL YEAR			
	2001/02	**2002/03**	**2003/04**	**%change over 2002/2003**
Murders	22	24	12	-50%
Attempted Murders	104	60	47	-22%
Shootings	99	113	136	+20%
Total Incidents	191	183	185	+1.1%

Table produced by operation Trident

The above table shows a substantial decline in murders and attempted murders within London over the past three years. However, other shootings have increased year on year over the same period. The figures show that consistently over the past three years there has been a shooting every other day in London alone. In the financial year 2003/04 one person was killed, along with four attempted murders, every month throughout the year. In the financial year 2003/04, there were twelve murders, four of which were cleared up. Indeed, the clear up rate is hampered by what the Police put this down, in part, to the general reluctance of the Black community to come forward as witnesses against the gunmen. I will not throw more statistics at you, but suffice to say that gun crime ever present in the Black Community. The previous Commander, in charge of Operation Trident, Alan Brown said: "The crimes investigated by Operation Trident have an impact on all Londoners. By acknowledging this and working with Local Authorities, we can ensure that there is a comprehensive response providing support to victims and witnesses. Those who are responsible for these crimes will be vigorously pursued, arrested and brought to justice."

VISUAL IMPACT

Just by way of comprehending the sheer scale of the problem of gun crime within the United Kingdom, in the illustration below I have allocated one star for each firearm related homicide of 2002/03 based on Home Office figures issued in January 2004:

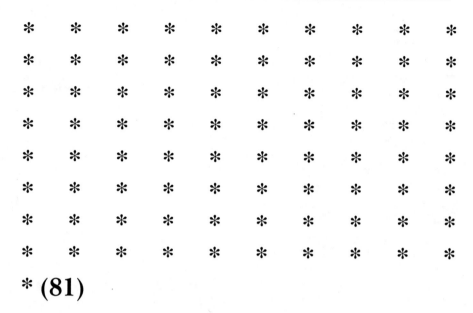

* (81)

Each one of these stars represent a tragedy, a loss of life, a family in anguish and mourning as a result of yet another pointless death. This is absolute madness.

INDEPENDENT ADVISORY GROUP

The Met set up the Independent Advisory Group to be a keystone of its strategy to tackle its failings in race related issues, as revealed by the McPherson report after the Stephen Lawrence murder. Local community support plays an integral part in Operation Trident. An Independent Advisory Group, comprising senior community leaders, helps to create a positive climate for members of Black communities to come forward with information about Trident-related criminal activity. The group is chaired by Lee Jasper, who is also Race Equality Adviser to London Mayor, Ken Livingstone.

TIP OFF

In one case, the police had received information from the public and had failed to pass it on to the appropriate department. Scotland Yard has admitted that an anonymous caller warned of the shooting at a London nightclub in Clerkenwell, early in 2003, but the details were not passed on to the right department. The information was given to Operation Trident; Trident then passed it on to the local police in Islington. The inevitable happened, a shooting did occur and a young man was killed. The question is what are we the community to make of this?

Early in July 2003, a massive police raid on North London communities sparked mixed reactions from residents. The pre-dawn dragnet saw more than 400 officers swoop in Harlesden, Kilburn, Wembley and Willesden, 13 men were arrested. The Voice Newspaper conducted a survey on the streets of Harlesden to gauge the response of the community to the operation. Many people were pleased the police had acted in such a forceful manner, although there was disappointment that they had failed to find any guns. This does, however, beg the question as to whether this is the type of forceful approach is necessary to win back the streets, and are we as a community ready to back it?

COMMUNITY RESPONSE TO CRIME

I have heard Black community leaders say "the Black man does not manufacture guns" and at the same time ask where are these guns coming from. I must admit when I hear such remarks, I recoil in agony of such a perpetual state of self-denial. We don't manufacture cars but we drive them, we don't manufacture planes but we fly in them. Surely its not the source of guns that's the primary issue, rather it is who has their finger on the trigger and what is in their heart. Other communities have access to guns yet they don't shoot each other mercilessly.

BLACK APOCALYPSE

The futility of gun crime is in itself abhorrent. Who gives anyone the right to take the life of another? Has life itself become so cheap within our community? Some of the shootings are conducted in public places, gangster style, with callous disregard for others. If we are not careful, as a community, we will find ourselves living in a type of "*dodge city*", a lawless city, out of control. If the rate of Black shootings were to be reflected in society as a whole, the UK would be in a state of emergency. Where then is this animosity towards each other coming from, what type of hatred or wickedness prompts men to do this? This is the challenge we face as a community and we can only begin to address it when we, as a community, begin to talk about it. There is evidence to suggest that we are starting to wake from our slumber. If these men had an understanding of their heritage or history, they would think twice about hurting each other.

Yet again another gun Amnesty meant people can hand in illegally held guns at local police stations and just walk away; no questions asked, no ID required, no fear of arrest, no fear of prosecution. This was an attempt to reduce the level of guns on the street, how successful this will be, only time will tell. The Government have introduced tough new sentences for those caught with firearms. But in order for this to be effective, the police will invariably have to stop and search. The question is; "are we prepared as a community to allow police to conduct stop and search, given our past experience? Do we now forget the pain of the infamous SUS laws of the past, in order to safeguard our physical security in the future?" In 2002, 97 lives were lost to gun crime, almost two lives a week. In 2003 however 81 lives were lost to gun crime a 16% reduction on the previous year according to Home Office statistics.

A MOTHER'S PAIN

Perhaps the best way to illustrate the futility of gun crime is to tell the stories of those left behind to mourn their loss. There can be no greater pain than that of a mother at the sudden loss of her child. However, when a child is lost to gun crime as opposed to illness, it is particularly devastating; mere words cannot express the pain and anguish a mother feels. One minute you have a child, the next minute the child's life has been taken.

Patsy McKie lost her son Dorrie to gun crime in 1999. Patsy McKie is such a mother; who was a founder member of 'Mothers Against Violence', which was at that time an organisation set up by mothers in the community. Patsy was told, by one of her son's friends, about other worried mothers in the community who were concerned about the level of crime and violence. Pasty's story is summarised below:

In the summer of 1999, on the day Patsy Mckie's son was killed, Dorrie (Patsy's son) meet up with a good friend who he had not seen for a while, and as a favour, decided to go out with him. Dorrie went in a car with two friends to basketball training. On the way home Dorrie was asked by the driver to accompany him to pick up some money. The other friend in the vehicle was later dropped off, prior to the incident. Dorrie and his friend then made their way to an address in a cul de sac, adjacent to a subway. Dorrie sat in the car whilst his friend went up to the house. Both Dorrie and his friend noticed they were being watched by several youths, who looked menacing. Dorrie's friend told Dorrie to get out of the car and run, but Dorrie felt, "why should he run as he had not done anything". Eventually, after more frantic encouragement from his friend, Dorrie decided to

make a run for it. The youths on bikes, wearing bandannas, gave chase.
Dorrie, who the family called Junior, was hit by three bullets, one of which
was fatal, and killed him on the spot where he fell.

Three young men were shot dead within a two-mile stretch of
South Manchester in the space of one week. McKie's youngest son,
Dorrie, 20, was one of them.

'Mothers Against Violence' firmly believes that everyone has a
gift. One key aim of the organisation is to try and get people to fulfil
their potential and to get young people more involved in finding the
solutions to their problems.

From the meeting with Patsy Mckie, it was clear that she is a
people's person, she takes a 'hands-on' approach when dealing with
youngsters. She is willing to challenge any youngster who is engaging
in anything, from anti-social behaviour, to being a gang member. Her
aim is simply to change their mindset and teach them to believe in
and love themselves.

Lucy Cope is a founding member of "Mothers Against Guns"
within the UK, and she has some interesting things to say about the
reality of gun crime. **DAMIAN COPE, Lucy's son,** was shot outside
a nightclub - a victim of gun violence. Lucy is determined her son's
death will not be in vain and, along with other mothers who have lost
children to shootings, is taking a campaign to end the killings to the
highest level. Here is Lucy Cope's story, in her own words.

Damian had been rushed to University College Hospital in central
London. He was critical. I had to get there fast. Driving through the empty
streets in the small hours of Monday, July 29, 2002. I came across a police
cordon around the nightclub in question in Holborn. I ran to the officers in
the street. I told them my 22-year-old son had been gunned down. A police-
man asked what his name was and I told him it was Damian Cope. I said
"Is he alive"? he looked at me, put his head back and said "He was when
he left there".

At the hospital I asked the nurse how Damian was and she said he was
very bad, he was critical, he had extensive bleeding. She said she'd update
me every 15 minutes and every time she came out my hope was just fading.
I knew that nobody could take so much and still survive. I called for the
priest. I asked for Damian to be given his last rights. I just said to the nurse
"Before you come and tell me, please make sure I get to see my son". I gave
her various messages to take to Damian, that I loved him and to give me
the strength to face what I had to face.

She was more or less, I feel, preparing me for when she did come out
and tell me there was no chance. When I saw her coming towards me and

she didn't have to say it. The very last time she came out I just knew by her face and she just very slowly nodded her head. I just said "Take me to Damian" and she did. I went in there and I could not believe it - I thought a couple of hours ago I saw this child on Burgess Park and now he is dead. I thanked him for fighting so long and I thanked him for the struggle he put up to stay with us. I said "I hope the person or persons responsible are caught" and then I held him and just turned around and walked away. There was nothing more I could do. "When I saw Damian in hospital, minutes after he was pronounced dead, I said he didn't look right. I could not find the right words to describe him but when I was driving back I just froze and started screaming. Then I knew what it was, it was fear. It had frozen on his face. I know my son saw his death coming because it was written all over his face and for that I will never forgive the man who killed him.

Lucy Cope is determined her son's death will not be in vain. She has joined anti-shootings organisation 'Mothers Against Guns' and hopes to take their campaign to the highest level. A White mother of black children, Lucy is outspoken of the gun culture that blights the Black community. Lucy believes tougher laws would crush the endless cycle of violence. She believes people caught in possession of a firearm should serve ten years behind bars with no parole. She also argues that gunmen should not be bailed on firearms charges and for the cold-blooded gunmen who take the lives of the innocent there should only be one sentence: life imprisonment with no parole. 'Mother's Against Guns' have called for the total banning of firearms.

At the time this book was drafted, a suspect had been apprehended for the murder of Lucy's son Damien, but when the case went to trial in August 2004, it collapsed due to lack of evidence.

On 30th March 2003 a memorial service was held for the families of victims of gun crime and for the local community to reflect, and pray, for the families and the community. It was organised by 'Southwark of Jesus' in support of, and alongside, Lucy Cope "Mothers Against Guns". A packed congregation came together in worship and bonding. Present at the church were Lee Jasper, the Race Advisory to the Mayor of London and Simon Hughes, MP. Lee Jasper spoke of a crisis amongst the youth, in that there are not enough youth centres, and a lack of attention from both teachers and parents alike. He went on to say that it is easy for criminals with large amounts of cash, to tempt disenfranchised youngsters into crime, particularly given the backdrop of high unemployment. Lee Jasper called for a return to traditional moral values, where fathers played a prominent role.

Simon Hughes spoke of the waste of life and the disease of violence and gun crime. He went on to say, that like any disease it can be over come with resistance, if the community stands together.

Church Ministers present at the memorial pointed out that they were now taking a more proactive approach to issues facing the community, they established a "late night club spot" where ministers go into nightclubs and attempt to reach youngsters. The church has also forged links with other institutions such as social services, in their attempt to intervene and provide some respite for those youngsters who are lost in a cycle of deprivation and crime.

Perhaps the most poignant part of the service was where mothers gave account of their suffering at the hands of gun crime. All the stories and accounts were indeed sad, but one story was so horrific that it touched my inner soul. This particular mother had come from abroad specifically for the memorial service. She had lost two sons to gun crime. Here is her story about the loss of one of her sons and her plight:

In November 1999, some local men living in the neighbourhood hatched this really wicked plan to target and rape her daughter. Three of these men were known to her as she had helped their mother to raise them. One of the men, who was there when the crime was being discussed, did not like what he was hearing and warned her daughter of this. Her daughter responded by staying with relatives, away from the family home. At that time she was unaware of her daughters plight, but being a woman of faith she had a strong premonition that something awful was going to happen.

One evening, as she lay in her bedroom watching television, she began to sob uncontrollably for no discernable reason. She had an innate feeling that something quite awful was going to happen, but as at the time she knew not what. The night in question she waited for her son to return home. When he came in she was relieved, he put his pushbike behind the door in the usual way. She, being a Christian, asked him to pray with her, he, in a matter of fact way, declined to do so and went to his bedroom. Later that night she was awoken by the front door being kicked, in rushed the gunman. "What do you want" she cried. The gunman rushed passed her, elbowing her twice in the face, as she clung on to him in a desperate attempt to stop him getting to her son. He marched straight into the son's room and shot him in the face, point-blank. He began to look furiously for the daughter, under the bed and in all the rooms. When he realised that she was not there, he turned the gun on the mother and asked for money. At that point she said "I only have loose change," he then pointed the gun to the side of her face and shot her. The bullet went through, dislodging her eye from its socket, leaving it resting on the side of her cheek. He then ran out leaving her for dead. She recalls how she clambered to the bathroom, attempting to wash the blood from her face, but the blood just kept oozing. When she managed to call help, the police exclaimed as they put her in the back of the jeep "this one is dead". When she arrived at the hospital, the doctor initially pronounced her dead. The police and staff standing over her could not believe it when her body started quivering, they were spellbound, it was someone else unconnected with the incident that summoned help and, as a result, she was revived.

If anyone had any doubts about gun crime, the above stories put it into perspective. I would urge parents who read this to encourage their teenage sons to read the above account of a victim of gun crime, so that they may fully appreciate the gory nature of the gun. If these mothers are prepared to share their experiences by giving such detailed testimony, then it is incumbent on us to listen and take heed. To my humble mind, is this not the real war, is this not the real front line, and is this not the real **terrorism**? Who was it that said 'Evil would prosper when good men keep quiet'? If this is our terrorism, where are our coalition forces that will search out the men of evil, and exact the requisite justice? If one lives by the sword, one can also die by the sword.

"Mothers against Guns" and "Mothers against Violence" have worked tirelessly for the cause and are doing great work, but the fathers appear to be absent and, it has to be said, this is a huge worry for the community. What a dichotomy, the young men are committing gun crime, and are also the victims of gun crime, yet their fathers are generally absent. Perhaps hidden in that scenario is the root cause of the problems we face today. Fatherhood is discussed in more detail later in this book, but what I will say is this, it is absolutely clear and unequivocal, a boy child without a father figure in his life is a potential bombshell, of which there can be no doubt.

What we have not discussed so far are the reasons why young men resort to gun crime. We already know that there is an inextricable link between social deprivation and crime and, as a community, we need to be mindful of that. What worries me is what is in the mind of a young man who chooses the gun as a solution to his problems. Later in this book I analyse the influence of Black music on our community. It is through music that I once heard the message that the young are trying to convey. The message is for those of us who open our ears and minds to listen, we may begin to understand the pain and suffering that some youngsters endure. We have to be receptive to the needs and wants of our youngsters and, incorporate them into being part of the solution. The question facing our community and society as a whole is how do we reach these young men and give them a sense of hope, turn their lives around in order that they can fulfil a useful role, not just within our community, but within the wider society? **It is perhaps worth noting that it is the young that hold the key to our future. I urge you to remember this, "the potential of a child is awesome."**

CRIMINAL CAMOUFLAGE SYNDROME

For those of us with children who are growing up at this time, this is the real dilemma as these children could inadvertently find themselves in the wrong place at the wrong time. Take the situation with the innocent young seven year old girl, fatally shot in the back in order that she could not identify her step father's killer. It is my view that the gun crime situation will get worse before it gets better. No one is immune from crime, therefore if we continue with the current level of inertia, we do so at our peril. A criminal can only survive in a society by hiding behind the law-abiding people in the community. A criminal needs to be invisible to the naked eye of law enforcement; they need to blend into society and the community and to take on the camouflage of being a law-abiding citizen. In the same way that the chameleon lizard camouflages itself; by taking on the colour of its surroundings to await its prey, at the same time avoiding detection from its predators. By hiding within the community in this way, the community as a whole could become stigmatised. It would be fair to say, therefore, that the criminal element amongst us, is hurting us as a community. I call it "the criminal camouflage syndrome", the transformation of a criminal to a law-abiding person and using the respectable people of the community as a shield.

We have heard the Government say they will be "tough on crime and tough on the causes of crime". This implies a double edged strategy; on one hand to deal with criminals in an affirmative way and on the other, to deal with social deprivation and poverty. But the fact remains that we are in danger of becoming a society of 'haves and have nots', and the Black community is over represented in the 'have not' area.

METROPOLITAN BLACK POLICE ASSOCIATION

The Metropolitan Black Police Association, has implemented a programme called 'Revival'. This is a programme of community initiatives created by the Metropolitan Black Police Association, in response to the rising incidents of gun and drug related crimes across

London and other hotspot cities in the UK. 'Revival' was launched during Black History Month, in October 2002.

The initiative aims to bring together communities, united in the struggle to reduce and eradicate drug and violent crimes. The objective is to facilitate the sharing of information and best practice regarding local community initiatives.

Director and creator of Revival, General Secretary Bevan Powell, said, "Revival, provides additional tools to help empower our communities address the growing use of guns and illegal drugs in inner cities. There is a crisis in our community! Gunmen are destroying families and creating fear. The police are tasked with keeping our communities safe, however, we all have a role to play in ensuring safer and healthier communities in our major cities".

THE EVIL WITHIN

One thing we must never loose sight of as a community,
is our civic and moral responsibility.
This is particularly acute when it comes to crime.
We must be clear and unequivocal in that we want the perpetrators to pay
with hard time.

No amount of government strategy or police initiative can compensate,
if inertia and apathy is our response, then as a community, we are sure to
deteriorate.

Crime in our community should be seen as the evil within,
it lurks and hides like a serpent whose sole intention is to sin.
A perpetrator that commits evil criminal acts,
and then uses the community to hide his tracks,
does not care whether the community is stigmatised or under attack,
as long as he manages to safeguard his back.

A criminal thinks about his own health and wealth,
which he does by dishonesty and stealth.
If what he does infringes our community,
it does not bother him, because he cares not for unity.

If we as a community want to live our lives with freedom and liberty.
We as a community must come together to fight 'the evil within' from a
position of consummate unity.
As a result 'the evil within' will have no hiding place or impunity.

Richard Todd

Drugs

INTRODUCTION

Illegal drugs have become a major industry *per se*. Traffickers, dealers and users alike flout the law on a daily basis. As drug gangs fight for lucrative turf, gun crime escalates out of control. The law of economics dictates that whilst drug supplies are limited, in that it is illegal, due to there illicit nature, the demand for them is high; the price of such drugs is as a result, also high, hence huge profit margins for those involved in the supply. However, like everything else in supply and demand economics when there are huge profit margins available to be had, there will always be more suppliers attracted to that market in order to take their slice of the cake, so to speak. A by-product of illegal drug use is petty crime. Drug users need to fund their habit and this, very often, can only be done through criminal activity. Street robbery, burglary and prostitution are typical means of a user who needs to fund a serious drug habit. Crack cocaine does pose a unique problem, its level of addictiveness is very high and its use appears to be growing at an alarming rate, particularly amongst the young.

DRUGS IN THE COMMUNITY

Like other communities we have an element within our own community that engages in the use of illegal drugs namely cannabis, marijuana also known as weed, ganga, herbs or spliff, and a host of other names, in the local vernacular. For many years now it has been the recreational drug of choice for some within our community. I recall, as a young man in the seventies one would go to parties and clubs where cannabis use was rife. Being a non-smoker myself I never really had an interest in it. If anything, in those days, I felt it was an impediment to one's ability to enjoy oneself when out on the town so to speak. Dealers would just come up to me and say "Weed boss" to which I would reply; "No boss". But then I would see friends that I had known from school buying it. I would watch them 'rolling up' in a meticulous way, using the index finger and thumb to roll (rizzla) the cannabis, as though it was a work of art. Then they would casually turn around and say: "Richie, you want a draw?" To which I always replied "No". They would look at me with astonishment, eyeball to eyeball and then say "Richie you sure?" To which I would always reply "Yes man I am sure".

I recall some of the popular musicians at that time sang about the use of cannabis in glowing terms, with lyrical content such as: *"From St Ann's it comes to you, the best collie weed you ever drew, so why should you run and hide, from the red seal the blue seal the concrete jungle too. Tired to smoke weed in a bush, tired to smoke weed in a gully, we want to come out in the open, but the breeze it blows it so far away, to the north to the south to the east and to the west"*. **Sang by the late Jacob Miller**. With the benefit of hindsight, I now see it was an appeal for the decriminalisation of cannabis; it was, perhaps, fifty years before its time.

The use of cannabis for medicinal purposes has recently been recognised by Health Professionals who believe it can assist in relieving the symptoms of <u>multiple sclerosis</u>. Others in the health profession suggest that long-term use of cannabis can cause mental health disorders. Later in this book I will discuss mental health care in more detail.

In recent years we have seen the proliferation of illegal and dangerous drugs within our community. Not only are there harder drugs being used within the community, but also the users appear to getting younger and younger. In the last ten years we have seen the introduction and expansion of the use of crack cocaine. The dangers of crack cocaine abuse are all too apparent, yet it has taken grip on our community, like leeches on flesh. Crack cocaine is a version of powdered cocaine, but crack cocaine is much more potent. It is cooked into a more concentrated version of the normal powdered cocaine. Crack cocaine is smoked, usually through a glass pipe. In the early eighties this drug dramatically hit the streets of the USA, since then it has had a devastating effect and has made a lasting impression on all major cities. Crack cocaine is one of the most addictive drugs on the streets.

Danny Kushlick of campaign group 'Transform'; said the Government needs to reassess its whole drugs policy, starting with the admission that making drugs illegal does not work. He said: "If you look at what happens when you hand the trade over to international, organised criminals and unregulated dealers you see all the problems the Government then tries to solve". So, turf wars; property crime; street dealing; access to drugs by young people, these are the problems that are actually caused by prohibition.

The various strategies we have seen from a range of would-be problem solvers vary between zero tolerance in Middlesborough, to the Lambeth experiment which saw the relaxation of the law regarding personal use of Cannabis. During the Lambeth (Brixton) experiment - introduced in 2001 by former Lambeth Police Commander, Brian Paddick - those found carrying small amounts of cannabis were given a warning by police, rather than being prosecuted. However, the Tories say that there has been a significant increase overall in drug trafficking in Lambeth and that drug dealers are in control, not the police. Kate Hoey, one of the local Labour MPs, has also condemned the experiment, saying it has made drug trafficking socially acceptable. Mr Paddick defended the scheme, saying there was no evidence to show his relaxed approach had attracted an influx of "drug tourists" to Brixton. Scotland Yard's Deputy Commissioner Ian Blair, said "the pilot scheme was undoubtedly beneficial to the police".

My only concern with the Lambeth experiment is why Brixton was chosen for such an experiment, for years now, Brixton has been seen as the spiritual home of the Black community. In choosing Brixton to conduct this experiment, is there not a tendency to link Brixton's Black community and drug abuse as being synonymous? I worry that it could be seen in the wider society as just that, which in turn may undermine us as a community and the way we are perceived by others.

PROHIBITION

Alcohol was once illegal in the USA (Prohibition). People still wanted to drink, however, and so the illegal supply trade grew, in order satisfy the desires of drinkers from all walks of life. Prohibition was a failure because the people liked drinking alcohol, and would break the law in order to carry on doing so. But before Prohibition was repealed, by a Constitutional Amendment, a huge criminal hierarchy had formed around supplying a substance that was once legal but which had become illegal due to an act of Congress. This is not an argument for decriminalisation; rather it is a statement of historical fact.

THE ECONOMICS OF THE ILLEGAL DRUG MARKET

The illegal drug market is no different to any other market in that where demand for a product exists, there will be someone there willing and able to supply the product to the market at a given price. This is basic economic theory of supply and demand. Demand, in an economic sense, is the willingness, backed by ability of an individual, organisation or entity, to purchase a commodity.

Fig. 1

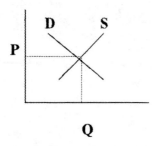

S = Supply
D = Demand
P = Price
Q = Quantity

Fig.1, shows that where supply and demand intersect this is the point which will determine the quantity of drugs supplied and the price to the market, otherwise known as the market equilibrium price, albeit an illegal market.

Much law enforcement attention has been focused on the supply side of the equation, but the demand for drugs remains relentless.

Fig 2

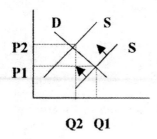

S = Supply
D = Demand
P = Price
Q = Quantity

Fig. 2, shows clearly what happens if supply to the market is limited by law enforcement seizures. The quantity of drugs supplied to the market is effectively reduced from Q1 to Q2, but the price goes up from P1 to P2. The spin off from this is that users will have to pay more for their drugs, they will become more desperate and could engage in more petty crime to fund their futile habit

Fig. 3

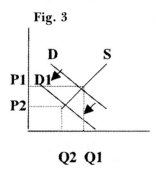

Q2 Q1

S = Supply
D = Demand
P = Price
Q = Quantity

Fig. 3, shows clearly that if demand is reduced the price will go down from P1 to P2 and, consequently, the quantity supplied to the market will decrease. This will make the trade less attractive for the suppliers, as profits will be reduced. The law of economics would dictate that any demand led strategies would, in the longer term, be more effective than any supply led strategies. This is a compelling argument to refocus the Government's anti-drug strategy on the demand side of the illegal use of illicit drugs.

Have some individuals within the community become so dissolutioned and, in want of escapism, to the point that some of us are willing to pay exorbitant amounts of money to get 'high'? Unless society can break the demand for drugs or legalise the supply of certain types of drugs, the problem is likely to increase. I would taper that by saying that legalisation of softer drugs, (Cannabis) is not without its problems, particularly the problem of progression. This is the possibility that people progress from soft drugs to hard drugs; particularly at risk from this are the younger users. The idea of taking the criminality out of the soft drug market and replacing it with appropriate health warnings may have some merit. I have heard it said in the past by financiers, that one can not buck the stock market;

perhaps hidden in that statement is the dilemma that faces the drug market. Notwithstanding this, I should point out that I am not advocating the decriminalisation of illegal drugs; I am merely articulating the debate.

We live in a society where we continually compete for resources, just think for a minute about your own achievements; did someone give you what you now possess? In reality you probably worked hard for what you have, in other words you competed for it, through employment or business, in one form or another. The reality of the situation is that not everybody is equipped to compete. Those that can not or do not want to compete, or who are strained by the need to continually compete, are at risk of seeking escapism through illegal drugs.

The drugs menace is here for the foreseeable future. So how can we mitigate the effects on our community? It is the responsibility of every parent to ensure that their child is aware of the dangers of drugs. If this means that we, as parents, must show our children the horror of drugs in all its gory detail, to see those who suffer the effects of drug abuse, then we must do so. Let them see how addicts live and, ultimately, how they die. We must remember it is our children who are the most at risk, as they represent future demand for drugs. **Kill the demand and, you kill the trade.**

My secondary school headmaster once said, "The best way to quit a habit is never to start". I would echo and concur with those sentiments. I am however, a realist and I do know that young people receive pressure from their peers to experiment. I also know that the more we tell young people not to do something, the more they are likely to want to experiment.

According to a recent Government survey, published in 2003, nearly half of all 15-year olds have tried drugs and one in five is a regular user. This survey canvassed 10,000 children from 321 English schools.

The Government has recently abandoned its drugs plan for schools and approximately half of England's drug advisors will be made redundant!

ILLEGAL DRUG USE

What is it about life that forces a young person to seek drug or alcohol intoxication,
whilst at the same time he or she frowns upon education?
It is as if they don't believe in 'deferred gratification'.
Is it to do with the lack of hope, or even the inability to cope?
Or could it be lack of self-esteem, that comes with the fading of a dream?

The drug market is demand led,
it is the reflection of a habit that needs to be fed.
Kill the habit and the drug market is dead,
keep the habit and it could be the user instead.

Remember this, give a man hope, help him to cope.
Reinforce his dream, bolster his self-esteem,
and he may, just may, stay absolutely clean.

Richard Todd

STREET CRIME

INTRODUCTION

Street crime and general anti-social behaviour, has become wide-spread amongst school children. It is cool or en vogue to behave like a thug. What starts as thuggish behaviour, can and in many cases does, lead to criminal activity. In a society where 'bling bling' is more important than education, where street credibility is more important than personal responsibility, there is a real danger that those who cannot afford to keep up are stigmatised by their peer groups. Street crime is not just confined to children; drug users and other opportunists will use the streets as a source of rich, criminal, pickings.

CRIMINAL METAMORPHOSIS

Children stealing mobile phones from others has become endemic. To steal leading brand named mobile phones using an intimidating and cold mode of operation, of simply walking up to a younger child and saying, "let me have a look at your phone" then removing the SIM card and just taking it, is evil. The fear of being caught does not enter the thieves heads. The poor victim left standing there, help-less and traumatised. In some cases boys surround their prey like wild animals, waiting and baiting for the kill. By stealing phones in this way, the boys will get so-called "ratings" from their peer group. The incidence of schoolboys stealing from other boys has reached epidemic proportions. A typical example is where an older boy will approach a younger, more vulnerable child, and say; "What have you got for me blood" or words to that effect. The thief often the older boy will then frisk the younger child taking whatever valuables he comes across. I call this "the thug-thief syndrome", it is happening all over our capital city. Another method of operation that seems to be gaining in popularity is where a group of schoolboys visits another, neighbouring school, with the sole intention to intimidate and steal.
   Boys visiting neighbouring schools spoiling for a fight is not a new phenomenon. What is new in recent times is the robbing, (mug-ging or jacking) of the victims. Other gangs target children on their

way home from school. They wait for the children to board the bus and then follow them upstairs in a cold and calculating way. Having secured the upstairs of the bus, military style, the gang will point to several victims and merely say "Phone" the victims, more often than not, hand over their mobile phones. This is dare I say, 'Highway Robbery'. This new development will have serious ramifications if allowed to continue unchecked. If this behaviour is not nipped in the bud, in a structured and forceful way, we will witness more serious crimes in the future which could end in someone getting seriously hurt. One father told me over a cup of coffee, that if anybody was to rob his child, providing his child could identify the perpetrator, he would deal with it. There will come a time when the father of the victim and the perpetrator will come into direct conflict and my fear is that the consequences could be fatal.

A child thief today is a potential gunman tomorrow, unless the crime cycle is broken. The pain and suffering this causes to the victim is incalculable, but the damage it is doing to us as a community, is staggering. When our children behave in a manner that brings our reputation as a community into disrepute, and we don't have anything to say not only as parents but as members of the Black community we inadvertently become part of the perceived problem. I call this "The Criminal Metamorphosis Cycle" where a child is growing up to be a criminal. I have heard it said that education is the key and, to some extent, I agree. But education is a longer-term solution, in the short term the problem still remains.

DRESS CODE

One phenomenon that never ceases to amaze me, is the large number of our youngsters who are wearing expensive designer clothes, yet they look positively untidy. Picture this for example; baseball cap perched on the head, covered by a hooded jacket; face barely showing, baggy trousers hanging half way down their behinds, gold and silver chains draped around their necks. Is this fashion, or is it an "I don't care" statement? Would you give such a young man a job, or let him into you house for that matter? Imagine if *we* feel that way about them, then what must others think? Yet these are *our* children, indeed *our* future. My simple advice to youngsters is this; '*if you want to be hired, make sure you're suitably attired*'. "*Fix Up, look sharp*".

LANGUAGE

The street language used is another limiting factor, for those who speak it at the expense of standard English. Perhaps the best way for me to explain the language used is to provide a glossary of the most widely used street terms.

Street terms	Meaning
Long flex	Long and boring
Shook	Afraid
Flossing	Spending money excessively
Buff	Attractive
Tick	Attractive
Bling bling	Big spender (sound of cash register)
Jack	Mug – (to rob someone)
Blood	Friend
Bro	Friend
Cuz	Friend
Fassy	Sissy
Safe	Thanks (OK)
Butters	Ugly
Heavy	Really Good
Beef	Conflict
Boyd	Disrespect/disregard
Seen	I Understand
Neek/Nerd	One who works hard, and/or does not conform to popular culture

The above list is not exhaustive, but it is an example of the language used on the streets. Some children cannot communicate without using one or more of these terms. They are unable to distinguish between street slang and standard English. I heard it said once that the wider the vocabulary we use, the better our thought process is in terms of generating ideas. This pidgin language adopted by the youth can only really be understood by others within that peer group. When these youngsters come into contact with institutions and organisations that require adequate command of English as the basic prerequisite for communication, these children find themselves unable to express themselves.

My sister who works in human resources told me she interviewed a 21 year old Black male for a job; he could not articulate to her what his skills were. She employed him anyway, as she saw a quality in him that perhaps others would not have seen. She found that he was skilled in information technology, but simply could not express himself orally. The point being if one cannot express oneself in standard English, one will not be able to sell oneself in the job market, hence an inability to compete.

GANG CULTURE

There is a school of thought that says gangs are born out of groups of young men who feel excluded from the mainstream. This is a reaction to the negativity that the mainstream society has placed upon them. The dress sense of some of our young men has been adopted from the USA, where gang culture is rife. Young Black men can no longer walk around with impunity. In the main, their adversaries are other young Black men. If a group of boys ventures into another area they could be set upon by other so-called gangs. It is futile, it is basic, but it is gang philosophy, respect plays a big part. But 'respect' does not have the meaning that you and I understand. Respect on a street level, means fear. One youngster told me that whilst he and his friend were walking home a group of young men came up to them and said, "yo bro what ends you mans from?" The youngsters had to think quickly on their feet, because if they mentioned the wrong area they would have been set upon. I pray this is not the beginning of US-style, gang turf doctrine.

In Los Angeles USA there is a notorious gang called "the blood" it is said that this gang inspired the low wearing baggy trousers dress code, after some of its members had been released from prison. Those members whilst in prison were not allowed to wear belts, hence there trousers rested on their behinds. This became dress code of the inmates and this was continued when they returned to the gang. The question I ask is as follows; Is this the role model for our young men? and, if this is allowed to continue will we see the type of gang violence in UK cities, that plagues the USA?

Outlined below is a Los Angeles Police Department LAPD table, showing the number of gangs and its members as at January 2003.

GANGS	NUMBERS	MEMBERSHIP
HISPANIC	204	30,864
CRIP	107	12,113
BLOOD	43	4,777
ASIAN	32	1,708
STONER	16	707

WHITE   5   878
TOTALS   407   51,047

The above chart portrays the scale of the problem in one state alone. The USA is about fives to ten years ahead of the UK in trend-setting. This is one trend, however which I hope is not emulated in the UK, but I fear the indicators suggest that we could be going down that road.

The police in Los Angeles (LA) are fighting an ongoing battle against gang violence. However, there are two police departments that have responsibility for law enforcement in LA the Los Angeles Police Department (LAPD) and the Los Angeles Sheriff's Department. Both of these forces have the same objectives but, in essence, they have different ways of going about them. The LAPD are hard and direct in their approach, whereas the Los Angeles Sheriff's Department relies more on intelligence about the gangs; they try to hack into the mindset of the gangster and in doing so, they have greater success. The Los Angeles Sheriff's Department has, on its home web page, a statement, which simply reads "Reaching the vision respect for diversity". Former New York Police Chief William Bratton, who pioneered "zero tolerance" policy, in the 1990s has been chosen by Los Angeles Mayor James Hahn as his new Police Commissioner. Mr Bratton, promised to liberate the Los Angeles force from the shadow of scandal and corruption and restore morale. Mr Bratton said he would "wipe clean" the reputation of the Los Angeles Police Department (LAPD) and that internal resistance to reform would become a thing of the past. Constance Rice a prominent US civil rights lawyer stated that the LAPD have deployed sweeping tactics, where certain groups in certain areas were stopped for minor violations. I must say this has a familiar ring to it.

The Greater Manchester Police, in association with other public sector agencies and community groups, have yet a different strategy to curb gang activity. The Manchester Multi-Agency Gang Strategy, (MMAGS), after receiving funding from the Home Office as part of the Targeted Policing Initiative, the MMAGS, was formed. It is an innovative approach, aimed at reducing the number of gang and gun-related crimes in Manchester and beyond, involving Greater Manchester Police, National Probation Service (Greater Manchester Area) and Manchester City Council. The underlying philosophy is to tackle those factors which lead to criminal gang involvement alongside tough law enforcement measures for those who continue to participate in criminal gang activity.

The Metropolitan Police state on their web site, "that a good Police service is one that reflects its community. Only through true understanding, trust and confidence can we work together to fight crime and build cultural bridges." The Positive Action Team (PAT) aims to encourage and support those from within the Black community who are currently under-represented within the Metropolitan Police Service. The question that even the Police themselves appear to be grappling with is this; "are the police, a force, or a service?"

We, as a community, must decide with the police, how best we want to be policed; we cannot sit back and leave it to others. We need to be fully involved in the solution to our problems. To this end we need greater transparency from the Police, in terms of how they intend to police the inner cities, what their success criteria is and, what results they have achieved. Much of this information is already available, but it is not in an easily understood format. We, as a community, in turn need to think deeply about how we relate to the Police. Yes, we have had negative experiences, but nothing is as negative as the wave of crime we are now experiencing within some parts of the community.

THE INFLUENCE OF BLACK MUSIC

The Black community have always had a close liaison with music. Indeed singing was one of the only joys a slave was allowed. If we look to the African American experience the music has always been at the forefront of their struggle. Listed below are different types of black music, along with names of prominent practitioners or exponents:

Work Song:	African Slave music.
Rag time:	Scott Joplin.
The Blues:	Muddy Waters, John Lee Hooker, Buddy Guy, Bessie Smith.
Jazz:	Louis Armstrong, Count Basie, Duke Ellington, Ella Fitzgerald.

We know from the rich tapestry of black music history, that music has always been central to the very core of our being. We cannot and should not therefore be surprised, when in today's society, music continues to play a central role albeit, that there has been a systemic change in the message conveyed by the music over the years.

It has been suggested that the music industry has undue influence on the young. The glorification of the gun and the subjugation of women is a direct attack on family values. The music industry is hugely powerful within the Black community; the large number of radio stations, which now play urban music, reinforces this. This is in itself worrying, in that all the stations play continuous music with little discussion about current affairs. The advertising associated with these stations is mainly for entertainment, i.e. where the next dance is, or who's having a birthday bash.

Whether we like it or not, some artists act as role models to our children. In recent years we have seen an explosion in the popularity of music videos, but the content of the videos is becoming more and more sexually explicit. Very often the artist is draped in jewellery and, if it is a male artist, young ladies usually crowd around him. If one thinks about it, they are trying to appeal to man's sense of sexuality and, judging from the success some of these artists are having, it appears to be working. Female singers also play the sexuality game; they dance in skimpy clothes, gyrating and showing cleavage. Men being men love to watch it, "sex sells" as they say, as long as women are prepared to strip and dance men are prepared to pay, as it appeals to man's most primitive urge libido. However, I do wonder what this does to impressionable young men, or women for that matter, in terms of their attitude toward relationships, sex and money, if these artists are their role models.

The lyrical content and body language of some of the music portrays anger and vexation. Some of the music even has a gangster connotation. Some of the male artists strut around the stage gesticulating, shouting and sometimes swearing. They may have good reason for being angry and they may be just expressing themselves; but what we have to be mindful of is how this is interpreted by the young and impressionable within our community.

I am not an expert on music, but in my opinion, the quality of urban music in full flow is, and has always been second to none. As youngsters growing up, we would only listen to two types of Black music; Reggae and Soul. Now there is Reggae, Ragga, R&B, Garage, Hip Hop, Rap and Gangster Rap, amongst others. This explosion of music comes with its in-built problems. The power of music can be used in a positive way to promote harmony and give guidance. Equally it can be destructive and promote slackness and greed. The problem we have, as a community is this, there is a danger that the lifestyle celebrated in this type of music may become a reality for our youngsters. Dare I say, our youngsters are caught up in an orgy of music.

We are a community, which needs to have a dialogue about the numerous problems that beset us, yet we demonstrate a level of inertia that borders on astounding. One radio station hosted what I like to call 'a dialogue weekend', which at the time, was a ground-breaking event, devoted to debates, discussions and phone-ins, to campaign against the rise of gun violence within the Black community in the UK, and especially London. Having said this, radio stations can do a lot more to help the problem, by refusing to play records which promote violence and excessive materialism. Some mainstream radio stations have already attempted this and most conscious listeners welcome the gesture. It is understood, however, that this could force such music underground. Notwithstanding this, it may well be a price worth paying as it sends out a positive message.

Even though much of the popular culture largely derives from the Black community, the community does not profit from it in a commercial way. The term "urban culture," in my opinion is a euphemism for Black inspired culture. Urban culture, Urban music; call it what you will. It has now been re-branded and re-packaged, sexed up and fed back to us in sizeable portions for a price. The price in case of the Black community cannot be measured in just money, we are paying for it with our souls. It is our community that is buying into it lock, stock and bling-bling barrel. Other communities look at it, watch it and enjoy it from a safe distance, they treat it merely as the light entertainment that it is.

Those within the community who are fortunate enough to be within the public eye, need to think about their responsibility to our community. The way we behave and act in public will inspire youngsters to follow the lead. Those who are successful must remember, that anything they achieve has an impact on the entire community.

GAIN REAL RESPECT

You use the language of the street.
You think it makes you complete.
You're into the latest fashion.
But with your education you ration.

When you go to school,
you are nobody's fool.
When you're out of school,
you care for no man's rule.
However now you're a man,
where the hell is your plan?

In your pursuit of quick monies,
you seek only to impress the honeys.
If bling-bling is your thing,
then you better believe later life will be grim.

As you look into your girl's eyes,
you feed her with those unnecessary lies.
You feel the grass is greener over there,
and if she questions you, you don't really care,
as you're more concerned with where you're going and what to wear.

Young man I notice your attitude to the gun,
you treat it as an fashion accessory for some fun.
If you mess about or tamper with ballistics,
you could end up being added to the statistics.
What is the legacy you have for your son,
if all you know is how to brandish a gun?

You have no concept of unity.
You have no love for our community.
Listen to your heart.
Listen to your head.
No time anymore, for you to be led.

Forget war and strife,
and start to lead a meaningful life.
Remember, you're a man with great prospect,
be a real man and gain maximum respect.

Richard Todd

CHAPTER VII

THE CRIMINAL JUSTICE SYSTEM

INTRODUCTION

It is vital for everyone to understand how English law enforcement works, as an entity, namely the Criminal Justice System. When individuals come into contact with the Criminal Justice System, it assists them if they understand the mechanics of the system. We, as a community, want to be assured that the Criminal Justice System is impartial and objective in the way it dispenses the law. For any civilised society, law and order must be a central plank. Just imagine for one minute if there was no law and order where would we be and what would society be like? The answer is, there would be some law and order; the law of the jungle, where only the fittest of the fittest survive. Business could not flourish, shops would be devoid of produce, the food chain would break down and hunger and starvation would ensue. Society as we know it would collapse. A sobering thought. Therefore we do need a Criminal Justice System that works and we should never lose sight of that. We have only to look at countries where the rule of law is compromised or corrupted, just picture the quality of life of those citizens living in those countries.

WHAT IS THE CRIMINAL JUSTICE SYSTEM?

The Criminal Justice System in England and Wales is comprised of several separate agencies and departments, which are responsible for various aspects of the work of maintaining law and order and the administration of justice. The main agencies of the CJS include:

1. The Police Service
2. The Crown Prosecution Service (CPS)
3. The Court Service
4. Magistrates' Courts
5. The Crown Court
6. The Appeal Courts
7. The Prison Service

8.　The Probation Service
9.　The Serious Fraud Office
10. The Criminal Defence Service
11. The Criminal Injuries Compensation Authority
12. Voluntary Sector

The flow diagram below outlines the maze of what is the prosecution system, or the judicial system:

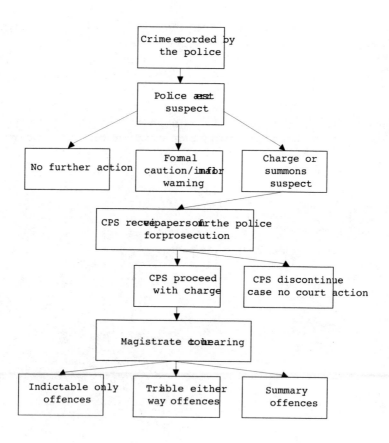

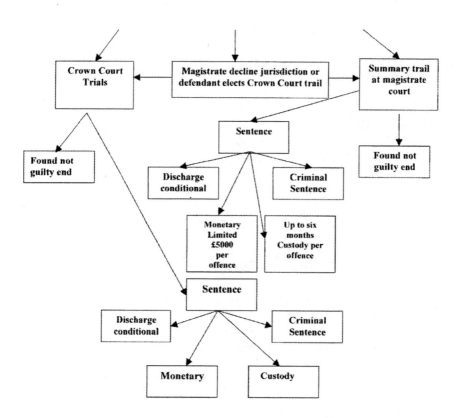

It is the judicial system that lay people have the most difficulty in understanding, which is why I have decided to show you diagrammatically, the way it operates, as an aid to comprehension.

The two key tenets of the criminal law in England and Wales are the presumption of innocence, and the burden of proof. The presumption of innocence means that an individual is deemed to be innocent, until proven guilty. The standard of proof required to find a defendant guilty in criminal cases in England and Wales is that the evidence should establish guilt 'beyond reasonable doubt'. This contrasts with the standard of a 'balance of probabilities' used in civil cases, where a person's legal liability is determined if the evidence suggests that the individual is more likely to be guilty than not.

The Home Office Minister John Denham, at that time 2001, called on all sections of the community to face up to racial discrimination and crime; as figures published have thrown a spotlight on race and the criminal justice system in the UK.

He also announced the introduction of interim minority ethnic recruitment targets for the Police service. The Home Office Minister said, he was keen that difficulties in recruiting ethnic minority officers in forces were identified early, so that they can receive appropriate help and support.

The Criminal Justice Bill 2003 has several key points through which it seeks to address what the Government sees as shortfalls in the current Criminal Justice System. Details of the main points are listed below;

1. Extension of Police Powers.
2. The Right to Trial by Jury.
3. Double Jeopardy.
4. Extending Sentencing Powers to Magistrates.
5. Previous Misconduct.

Whether any of these measures singularly or in together can deliver a more cohesive and transparent Criminal Justice System is debateable. I am always guarded against more Police power, if such power is without transparency and accountability. When you read the chapter on "My Experience of Law Enforcement", you will perhaps see and understand where I am coming from on this matter. What is clear, however, is that the Government is trying to toughen up the system towards the criminal and, to be honest, that has to be something we in the community would welcome, with particular regard to serious crime.

The Government has taken important steps in recent years to tackle racism, including implementation of the Race Relations Amendment Act, which requires public sector agencies to demonstrate how they will promote race equality for their staff and for the public they serve. The Government has emphasised that it is now time to move forward to meet the challenges ahead and build on these firm foundations. To ensure that Government policies work correctly and in the right direction, supporting the premise of racial equality, the Home Office has listed what the Government see as being the underpinning principles of community cohesion. They are that:

*   There is a common vision of a sense of cohesion for all communities.
*   The diversity of different peoples' backgrounds and circumstances are appreciated and positively valued.
*   Those from different backgrounds have similar life opportunities.

- Strong and positive relationships being developed from people of different backgrounds in the workplace, schools and within the neighbourhood.

The Government recognises that the scales of justice are weighted heavily against the Black community. Having recognised this they have taken some measures in an attempt to try to redress the situation. Many of us have had negative experiences at the hands of the Criminal Justice System. I have often heard people within the community say that when a Black man appears in front of the judge, he is going down. That is to say that he will receive harsher sentencing than his White counterpart. There is now a body of evidence that would tend to support this view, which the Government have now recognised.

Research on ethnic minority confidence in the CJS shows a mixed picture. A study commissioned by the Central Office of Information explored confidence in the CJS among minority ethnic communities in England and Wales and found that ethnic minority communities shared broadly the same perceptions of the CJS as do the rest of the population. The common view is that the same system is too soft on criminals, and the needs of the victims were often not met. In addition, it was felt that elements of the Black community were viewed as a criminal underclass by the CJS.

According to 'Nacro', (a leading crime reduction charity), every year, prison statistics show that Black and Minority Ethnic (BME) groups are over-represented in prison. The latest figures show that BME groups make up 21% of the prison population, yet only 9 % of the general population outside of prison. Nacro go on to say that there is no sustainable evidence that Black minority groups are more prone to commit crime than White people.

The Royal College of Psychiatrists carried out a study in December 2002, of ethnic differences among prisoners. The key findings relating to criminality and psychiatric problems were:

I. The rate of imprisonment is six times higher for Black than for White men and women.
II. Black male prisoners were more likely to be charged with or convicted of, robbery and firearm offences; there were no differences for other categories of offences such as; homicide, major violence, sex offences or burglary and theft.

I am deliberately not going to say a lot about the penal system in this book. Not because I don't consider it important, but because I do consider it so large and diverse a topic that I would have to conduct extensive research before I could do it justice. It is however, something that I am considering for the future.

CRIMINAL JUSTICE

Crime is the scourge of any civilised society.
Therefore we need a Criminal Justice System that has transparency and
integrity.
To uphold the rule of law,
Is all that we are looking for.

Just think, without the Criminal Justice System we would have anarchy.
With the Criminal Justice System we have a certain level of sanity.
We want a Criminal Justice System we can trust,
so that we can move away from years of mistrust.

We can not change the system from outside,
we must look to reside inside.
Justice and equity is all we seek,
lets face it, without it the future is bleak.

Richard Todd

CHAPTER VIII

MY EXPERIENCE OF LAW ENFORCEMENT

INTRODUCTION

The general perception of the mass-media is that the Black man is more likely to offend than his white counterpart and, the general public concurs with this view. This, I believe, is largely due to the atavistic racial imagery portrayed by the mass-media. The flip side of this is that the innocent Black man is more likely to be stopped by the police whilst going about his lawful business than his White counterpart. I believe my experience to be an example of what has happened to many law-abiding Black men over recent decades, which is why I feel the need to share it with you, the reader and at the same time get it off my chest.

The Police would argue that they have taken great pains to change since the 70's and, to be honest, I do not doubt that. I would even go as far as saying that policing has become more difficult and problematic in recent times. The proliferation of gun crime and the spectre of terrorism have impacted on policing in a way that, perhaps, we could not have envisaged as recently as 10 years ago. This particular chapter is about my personal experience, my reality and, the reality of many others who just want to go about their lawful business without aspersions being cast upon them.

RED ROVER

In the past, Black men, have had their own experiences of the law enforcement institutions and, I must confess most of the experiences have been negative. My first encounter with the police was as a 14 year-old. Back in those days one could buy what we now call a 'travel card' (Red Rover). It was a day on the buses, any London Transport red bus. We would board a bus simply to see where it would take us. It was a fantastic way to see London with a youthful spirit of adventure, coupled with the belief that if one did no wrong, then one would suffer no wrong from the hands of the Police. On the day in question, we were on a No 37 bus in Clapham Common, when we decided to get off. As the 4 of us got off the bus and crossed the road, a policeman walked briskly up to us. He asked us where we were going, to which we replied "we are catching a bus", which was true. To my amazement he then said "hurry up we don't want your sort here. Get back to Brixton". The irony was none of us came from Brixton, and Brixton was only at most, two miles away. So we just got on the bus and when he had gone we started laughing. Whilst this in and of itself may not have been a major issue, it was an indicator of the mental attitude of some Police Officers at that time. It was to mark the beginning of a series of many similar experiences with the Police during my adolescent years. However, not all experiences with the Police were negative, but as a young man, when you feel you have been wronged, you tend to remember it.

THE PRODUCER SYNDROME

As a teenager in the 70's I was stopped countless times whilst driving, going about my lawful business. In one year I was stopped no less than 20 times. For the majority of these spot checks I had to provide proof of car insurance and motor vehicle road worthiness (MOT), the so-called producer, yet no criminal or other charges were ever levied against me, as a result of such stops. Every time I was stopped, the Police officer would ask, "Is this your car"? On one occasion I was stopped I asked the Policeman; "why?" He just replied, "Your face looks like a criminal". Even a reggae artist (Smiley Culture) produced a record, which included the lyrics "Police officer don't give me producer". It was happening so often in our community, it became a standing joke. The record used humour to highlight a serious situation. Oddly enough, the 'producer syndrome' was to curtail after the riots in the Eighties.

BRIXTON RIOTS

On the evening of one of the Brixton riots I was at a friend's flat, we were planning that evening's entertainment. We heard the sirens but we paid them little attention until we looked out the window and saw herds of people running, pursued by the Police. It was then that I realised that this was something out of the ordinary. That day I saw bottles and dustbins flying through the air, aimed at the oncoming Police. Cars were being bounced up and down like yo-yos, then turned over and used as barriers. When I saw that, my immediate concern was for my car; albeit not much of a car, nonetheless, it was my pride and joy. I decided that I needed to get the car quickly and go home but, when I went for the car, to my horror, it was in an area cordoned off by the Police. "Nothing in and nothing out" they exclaimed. It meant I had to take the bus home, but no buses were running through the affected area. So I walked through the carnage. The sound of windows being smashed, sirens going, fires blazing, the smell of smouldering rubber burning, people screaming, along with the Police running around looking like paratroopers, was not only disorientating but also frightening. I managed to walk through the Police cordons and on to a place where I could take a bus home. The whole experience felt surreal at the time, whilst I was seeing what was happening before my very eyes, mentally I could not comprehend it. Yet I had a strange sense of foreboding and helplessness, as well as a sense that some good may come from this bad situation.

I remember walking through Brixton the day after the riot, to go and retrieve my vehicle. As they say; "After a storm must come a calm". It was a sunny Sunday morning and calm had been restored. I recall the smell of burning vehicles, roads blocked by burnt-out cars lined out across the road, and shop windows completely destroyed, their contents looted. I saw police strategically positioned through-out Brixton and, surrounding areas, supported by other police who remained in their coaches and minibuses, in readiness for any re-oc-currence. If Brixton was the spiritual home of the Black man at that time, then our home had been gutted; and that is exactly how I felt. I hope and trust that I never see that sight again.

Another incident that particularly stands out in my mind was when I was stopped whilst boarding a bus in the early 1980's on my way to college. I had one foot on the bus when a Policeman asked me to step off the bus and show him what was in my bag. To which I replied; "I do not want to be late for my lecture" and refused to get off the bus. Why should I get off the bus I thought, I am just going about my lawful business. However, I did open my bag for inspec-tion on the bus, much to the frustration of the passengers who were disgruntled as they too were inconvenienced. The Policeman found only college books to his obvious disappointment. Strangely enough the passengers, most of whom were White were supportive when they realised what was happening. I must admit, I found this unlikely sup-port reassuring.

CRIMINALIZING THE INNOCENT

The straw that broke the camel's back came with an incident that happened to my younger brothers. One was sixteen years old the other thirteen at the time. The older of the two had taken an examination on the morning in question and, as a reward, was allowed to go to Hamley's (toy shop) in the West End of London, and was to take our younger brother. My mother gave them the usual behavioural instruction, along with a time by which they should return home. That evening when I arrived home from work, I saw my mother in a distressed state. "The boys have been gone since 1pm", she stated, "and I am very worried". We were about to start phoning around, when we received a phone call from the Police, stating that the boys were being held at a police station and that they had admitted attempting to steal a woman's purse, and we were to come to the station. The two minors were in fact interviewed without an adult present. The younger of the two was told that he would not see his mother again if he did not admit to the alleged crime, which he clearly did not commit. I remember my father stating in anger, "Whatever it takes financially, I am going to find the best lawyer to fight the case because this is wrong". Up until that point, my father was supportive of the Police, the incident was to change his view drastically. When the case came to the Magistrate's Court and the police saw that my parents had engaged the services of a barrister, they hurriedly asked for the hearing to be adjourned in order that they could better prepare their case. When the case was eventually heard, the Police offered flimsy circumstantial evidence; they had no victim, and no prima facie evidence. The Headmaster of the boys' school came to court and gave a character reference. He stated that the boys had never been in trouble at school and that they were indeed, good pupils. The Magistrate when summing up pronounced that; *"the boys had acted out of character"* and they were bound over to keep the peace. It was clearly not the success that the police were looking for; nor was it the acquittal that we were looking for! I remember looking over at the Police officer after he presented his evidence; he never once looked in the direction of my family. The Magistrate's summing up, I felt, was a euphemism for saying; *"I know you did not do it, but we must save face for the Police"*. I say if time is the master then let the master speak for himself. The boys had never been in trouble before, nor were they after the incident. Some twenty-five years later, and they are both professional men with **no criminal record**. In fact no one in the family has a criminal record. I would suggest that the facts speak for themselves. What I learnt from the above stated incident was that the Police did not have a clue when it came to dealing with Black youth at that time. They were either unwilling, or unable, to differentiate between a criminal and a well-behaved person. What was alarming at the time was the fact that they drew some basic incorrect assumptions about the boys, which were completely wrong. At best I would describe it as lazy policing, at worst it was a blatant disregard for equity and justice in the pursuit of a conviction.

One day in the mid-eighties, my brother and his good friend, went shopping and on the way back decided to place a bet in the local turf accountant's. They promptly went inside, sat down, put their shopping down and sought to place their bets. They were only in there a few minutes when the door burst open and in came a stream of armed Police. My brother and his friend were asked not to move whilst the Police rummaged through their shopping bags. When the Police officers were asked why they were doing this, they simply replied "Don't worry about it." When the Police found nothing they just turned around and left, no explanation and no apology. Outside the turf accountant shop, a cordon of police lay in wait in the event of any trouble. When I visited the Police station later that day to ask for an explanation, I was told in no uncertain terms to go away. Both of the young men in question went on in life to professional careers as an IT Professional and Architect respectively. Sadly my brother's friend, who ultimately became a close friend of the family, is no longer with us. I know however, that if he were alive today, he would fully endorse what I am saying, because that was his nature, as a professional man. The most harrowing thought, regarding the incident, was that two innocent young men could easily have been shot if things had gone disastrously wrong, as in the Dorothy Cherry Groce shooting. This was a case where the Police shot and injured a mother of six, which in turn sparked riots in Brixton in the Eighties.

My wife and I were on our way home from shopping in the early 1990's. As we drove homeward to our amazement a car turned right, into an oncoming cyclist. The motor vehicle clipped the cyclist, throwing him off his bike and to the ground. The driver of the vehicle did not stop; he/she just drove off. My wife and I were absolutely horrified so we stopped and asked the victim if he was alright. He was clearly in shock and some considerable pain. Fortunately, someone phoned the ambulance and they were quickly on their way. A few minutes later we heard Police sirens, they rushed over to the incident and took one look at me, clearly making up their minds that I was responsible. I told the Policeman it was not me, I was merely assisting the victim. It was not until the injured person, in his pain and agony, explained to the Policeman that it was not me, that they decided to refocus their attentions. By the time the Police decided to ask me about what I saw, I was so disgusted that I got back in my vehicle and drove off.

FISH BOWL SYNDROME

Just by way of anecdotal illustration, as a means of demonstrating the perception of a Black man. I recently recall sitting outside a shopping centre in my car with my 17 year-old son, chatting as we usually do, waiting for my wife to return from the local supermarket. When we noticed, to our horror, that we were attracting attention from the general public, despite the fact that we were sat talking quite innocently and glibly. As people walked past they would stare, as if we were in a fish bowl. Shop security guards would look, meticulously taking the registration number of the vehicle. My worst fear was that if something were to have happened in the vicinity, we would have found ourselves having to be eliminated from Police enquiries. This in fact happened on two separate occasions, one of which resulted in my being asked to provide a DNA specimen, whilst I was on my way to pick up my daughter from school. In fairness to the Police, they were polite, and they went to great lengths to explain why they stopped me. However I still felt aggrieved. Why should I have been stopped whilst going about my lawful business, on the public highway? Eight weeks later the Police wrote to me and thanked me for my help and that I am now eliminated from their enquiry, and that the voluntary DNA sample would be destroyed. I am still aghast as to why I should have been subjected to that indignity. The question I would raise is, "Have we done this to ourselves as a community and are we partially to blame for the way the general public perceive us? or is it just prejudice and ignorance from the police and some of the general public?"

Are we not, therefore the silent victims of those within our community, who seek to perpetrate crime? Whilst they may escape justice, the community cannot hide. One friend once told me **"As a community, it is the few bad that make it difficult for the many good"**. In my view never has a truer word been spoken. This general perception does not stop on the streets, the mistrust of the black man is echoed in the work place, although it is more subtle in nature, and in some cases only visible to the trained eye.

POLICE STOPS 2004

The Police have stopped my son, who has been driving for only twelve months, at least sixteen times over that period for spurious reasons. I own the car and I insure the car for him, but he seems to fit their stereotype of a likely criminal. They have no knowledge of his background, one has to assume that he fits the profile of what they consider to be a high-risk group. The car has to be in tip-top condition at all times, all lights working etc. He can give no possible reason for the police to stop him, because if the Police find an excuse to stop him, they will. The questions I would ask are, "At what point does this become an infringement of his 'Human Rights'? or "does he have to go through the same hardship I did 27 years ago?"

One of the key pennants of the Criminal Justice System is the presumption of innocence until proven guilty. But, given my personal experiences as outlined above, this essential pennant of the Criminal Justice System appears to be completely overlooked. Rather, the contrary would appear true, guilty until proven innocent, when dealing with a certain section of the community. *If you're in the wrong place at the wrong time, you have to prove you're innocence.*

Nacro is a Voluntary Sector Organisation working in crime prevention and providing services for ex-offenders. A Nacro online editorial stated that, stop and search figures do not support 'political correctness' claims" Stop and search has a limited impact on crime, but has a massive impact on community relations. It is also a blunt instrument. Despite improvements in the arrest rates, a large majority of those stopped and searched by the Police are not subsequently arrested". Nacro also stated in its autumn 2003, 'Race for Justice' publication, that: nobody in the minority ethnic community believes that the complex arguments which are sometimes used to explain the figures for stop and search are valid'.

Nacro believes that the Criminal Justice System must serve ethnic minority communities more effectively if it is to deliver justice fairly and promote confidence in its performance.

It is well known that minority groups are disproportionately represented in all areas of the criminal justice system, *as suspects, defendants and offenders*

- Statistically, young Black people are stopped and searched eight times more often than young White people.
- The inmate population of prisons in England and Wales contains five times the number of Black people found in the population at large.
- Black people found guilty of offences are more likely to receive custodial sentences, often longer sentences, than their white counterparts.

COMMUNITY EXPECTATION

We, as a community, are entitled to fair treatment from the Criminal Justice System, a system that's oblivious to sex, race, colour or disability in the practice of law. One way to improve confidence in the Criminal Justice System to employ more Black staff in all areas of the institution. The Home Office has begun to set targets for the employment of Black staff. We as a community, however, need to be assured that;

1. The targets are reasonable.
2. There are systems in place to achieve the target.
3. There is a proper mechanism in place to capture data relating to CJS employment.
4. There are periodic meetings between CJS management and the community representatives, to discuss progress.

DIVERSITY IN THE POLICE FORCE

The idea of racial diversity in the Police Force has been around for a long time. The Scarman report of 1982 included the following statement: "There is widespread agreement that the composition of our Police Force must reflect the makeup of the society they serve. A Police Force, which fails to reflect the ethnic diversity of our society, will never succeed in securing the full support of all its sections". The report of the Stephen Lawrence Inquiry mirrors the view that Police forces should be representative of the communities they serve.

As a young man I remember, the distrust that vast members of our community had for the Police, but, in my view it was not without due cause. I even remember members of the Police Force saying they did not want to lower their academic standards for the recruitment of ethnic minorities. That proved to be a flawed argument, because many of us went on to be professionals, in other fields. Many of us felt we were being traitors to the cause if we even began to think of employment within the Police. With the passage of time and much gained experience, we must leave behind shallow thinking, to look wider, in terms not only of our community but the betterment of the wider society. To this end, we should encourage our youngsters to apply for employment within the Criminal Justice System, as they consider appropriate. A Criminal Justice System that reflects the community it serves will strengthen confidence in the system.

Lastly, it would be prudent if more Black professionals were to explore the possibility of becoming Magistrates. A Magistrate does not have to be a qualified lawyer, quite the contrary; they merely have to be of good professional standing.

STOP CASTING ASPERSIONS ON ME

Why do you cast aspersions upon me.
When all I want is for you to let me be.
I am sick and tired of your notions and preconceptions.
How do you know what's in my head and my intention?

I toiled so hard to make it,
but you think that, somehow, I've faked it.
If you don't talk to me, how can you even begin to know me.
The first thing you see when you look at me, is the colour of my skin,
you don't see who I am, what I have done, and where I have been.

On my way to work, I stepped out my front gate.
When I noticed two policemen watching, I knew my immediate fate.
"Where are you going they politely asked"?
"I am going to work to complete an audit task"
"Where do you work and where do you live", they asked.
"I work in the city, and if I am late for my meeting, it would be a real pity,
and I live over there, you can check if you care.
I'm just going about my lawful business I have nothing to fear".
After much delay they said, "thanks for your co-operation and help sir"
I replied, "now I am late, it is a lift to the station that I would prefer"
"Sorry sir we are inundated with work and very busy"
I thought, if you're so busy why the hell did you stop me,
its things like that that make me dizzy.

Is this the price we pay for policing today,
in this most unscientific way.
They cast out their fishing net, far and wide;
whilst innocent men like me have to abide,
in a vain hope that crime they will detect,
but it is our people that suffer the adverse effect.
Whatever happened to the slogan 'to serve and to protect'.

When I walk down the road,
I feel that on my back there is a heavy load.
I want to be free, like a bird in a tree,
However I know you are watching and casting aspersions upon me.

Richard Todd

CHAPTER IX

THE FAMILY STRUCTURE & HEALTH

INTRODUCTION

There is, without doubt, a breakdown of Black family values; there are now more dysfunctional Black families than ever before. This is where the mother and father of a child, for one reason or another, are not together, or if they are together they are chaotic. This is not just true of the Black community but also of society as a whole. Traditionally the Black woman has acted as the backbone of the household, particularly with regard to the raising of children. Some say, this is a legacy of the slave trade, where men were routinely parted from their families. However, with the increasing number of teenage parents many, children are being brought up in a less structured environment. A teenage parent, working hard, may not be in a position to focus on the needs and wants of the child. Alternatively, the young parent may not be working, perhaps living on income support, with the obvious financial implications that situation has. Needless to say, some children are raised without a positive, male, role model in their lives. Single parents in professional positions, with support from their extended families, do not tend to fall into this category.

A CHILD'S PLACE

Children nowadays want to be in 'vogue,' they want the adulation of their peer group, they want to grow up before their time; they are in a hurry for adulthood. Yet at the same time they are not ready to accept adult responsibilities. Countless times I have visited homes and seen their little child still are running around after 10pm at night. Is this the beginning of indiscipline? Could this be tomorrow's lout? I remember my parents saying to me; as a child, "you're a child and as a child you must maintain a child's place". Imagine telling a child that today; indeed, what is a child's place? In the old days a child's place was clearly defined, "To be seen but not heard". Today that might be seen as a form of mental abuse. If adults were speaking, you dared not get involved in the conversation, unless you were asked to. Today is about freedom of expression. Children have the upper hand, they can say anything, do anything, and behave in any way without consequence, without fear of discipline. I have often seen children no older than twelve playing on the street as late as 11pm at night. I often wonder, with some despair; "Where on earth are the parents?" To coin a Jamaican phase we would call them *"let go beast"* which basically means they're left to their own devices, to run wild.

The lack of respect exhibited by some children towards adults is disheartening. I have mentioned this already in this book but, because I feel it is of such importance, I will mention it again. Any society or community where neither the children or young adults respect the elders, is heading for catastrophe. It is the elders that have the experience, wisdom and knowledge. Failure to take that into account would suggest that the youngsters are destined to make mistakes in life that could easily have been avoided. There is an old Jamaican saying *"Hard ears children, bite rock stone"* which means if a child does not listen to responsible adults, they will run the risk of making mistakes that could have been avoided. Some adults are now afraid to speak to children, out of fear of their own safety or fear of abuse. I saw a situation once when children were behaving badly on a bus. A good citizen asked them; "Please behave yourselves." The girls, who could not have been more than thirteen, replied, "what, shut you mouth fool before I wet you up with my drink, what, what". The girls took a confrontational approach to what had been a reasonable request. In another case, which was heavily reported on recently, around 50 school girls between the ages of 12 and 16 were involved in an ugly confrontation with British Transport Police who were mounting a crackdown on ticket-less travel and bad behaviour. The Police claimed that the girls were screaming, kicking and scratching like banshees.

In one specific though not isolated case, a 14-year-old girl who craved peer group respect, kept threatening another child who was in the same year at school. The girl had the audacity to text the other child with abuse and threats. When the victim's parents saw the nature of the texts they decided to take direct action. They phoned the girl back immediately and said "Please don't phone or text my daughter, just leave her alone". In speaking to the girl they noticed her attitude and demeanour was curt and abrupt. They wrote to the school and asked them to deal with the matter. If they had been hot headed, the outcome could have been quite different. The point is, this behaviour has become widespread, clearly one day this could and probably will lead to a serious incident. Most parents give their children phones as a safeguard, to know where the child is, and for the child to be able to contact their parents if need be. In practice, however, the phone is seen by children as a status symbol, and is used, in the most part, for idle chitchat and seemingly pointless texting. Where technology and bad behaviour are fused together, they conspire to create new problems for parents, instead of providing solutions.

Some of our children wander the streets aimlessly, shouting, screaming, swearing and in some cases, spoiling for a fight. The worrying thing about all this is that the children genuinely believe that there are no consequences to such behaviour. No society can function effectively unless rules and regulations are observed and preserved. A society without rules and regulation will in the longer term, restrict the freedom of the individual. It is an inherent part of parenthood to impart the values of good citizenship, good manners and etiquette. Trevor Philips, the Chair of the Commission for Racial Equality said in a television interview that his father would always say "*manners maketh the man*". I honestly believe that a level of courtesy and good manners is the first port of call on the way to good citizenship.

FATHERHOOD

The term "baby father" has become synonymous with Black single-parent families. The term "baby father" has replaced husband and partner and perhaps typifies the changing times. The meaning of fatherhood, to some Black men is the same as vanity. They believe that because they can stand up vertically and horizontally they are men. Sorry to quote the same old cliché, but "any male can a biological father a child, only a true man can be a real father." Far too many men are ducking their prime responsibilities with regard to their children. Some fathers are quite simply not there for their children, as they grow, the very time the child needs them most. They see raising children as a responsibility they can do without. Others think by paying child support, they have discharged their responsibility. Some men are just 'players' for life, but I say don't hate the 'players', I just hate the game they play. If a father fails to bond with a child whilst that child is growing up, then it is almost impossible to form a bond with that child once that child reaches maturity. Having said this, there are many Black men, who live up to their responsibilities providing focus and direction for their child or children.

The lack of a positive, male, role model in the lives of so many of our young men is a real issue for us. Some boys have only really known their mothers and cannot even when given the opportunity, relate to their absentee father. With the greatest respect to single mothers, when it comes to raising boys, they do find it challenging, vis-à-vis discipline. I hear and understand women when they say "I' am an independent woman and I don't need a man" and there may well be some truth in that, but it is not necessarily the woman that needs the man, it is the child that needs both parents; in particular a boy child needs a father figure. As a child I remember being told by my mother; "You wait until your father gets home", I tell you, those immortal words were frightening! Any notion I had, about being rude or misbehaving, was quickly and un-surreptitiously expunged. This effect was not unique to me. I remember my school friends worrying about what their fathers would do under certain circumstances. As a teenager I could not just pick myself up and go out and come in at all hours, there were household rules to be observed, some of which I observed and, some I didn't and I faced the consequences. Contrast that with the reaction from children today; if one says to them "I will tell your parents," their response is more likely to be, "Go on then". As far as the child is concerned; there is little or no consequence, there is no price to pay for indiscipline and rudeness. It is that lack of fear of consequence that is at the heart of the rudeness and indis- cipline exhibited by children today.

One colleague of mine described the syndrome as 'payback time'. By that he meant it was a result of the eighties where relationships were more casual, as was sexual encounters. Young men and women would meet in clubs or at parties; no one thought about the long- term implications, all that was on their minds was the immediacy of their encounter. I had the privilege of growing up on a feast of good reggae music, at the time when the late Crown Prince of reggae, no other than Dennis Emmanuel Brown, was in his hay day. He sang records like, "no man is an island", "baby don't do it", "silhouette", "if I follow my heart", "stop the fussing and fighting" and many more. The vocals were clear and the lyrics clean and pristine, the content was silky and mellow. When the music hit the party people, as men held women in a tight embrace, some men using the walls within the building structure to support their backs, they would simply shout out in their delight "Rewind selector" in a vain attempt to influence the disc jockey in the hope that he might restart the record, in or- der that they could continue the dance. At that particular time, they were captured in the heat of that moment; any objective thinking had long since gone, i.e. they were feeling the vibes. Those of you that have been there, will instinctively know what I am talking about, others will have to trust me on this one. Dare I say, one thing leads to another.

Sex was always high on the social agenda. With the sexual revolu- tion of the sixties came the notion that all was fair in love and war, which continued into the seventies and eighties. I remember speaking to many friends and old schoolmates, who would take great pleasure in announcing that their "woman", as they put it, was having a child. They would then go on to say "But we are no longer together" for one reason or another. Hence, the infamous 'absentee father'.

MISSPENT YOUTH

I've seen many a young man sharp, quick witted and proud,
I've seen him, effervescent, lively and loud.
The way he behaves, he'll always stand out in a crowd,
but little does he know, that over his head hangs an ugly cloud.
He does not know that youth is a gift from the Almightily,
instead he runs around and takes everything lightly.

When he was young his Mother told him" its time to settle down,
and stop this stupid running around."
He replied, " this is modern times mother;
but with serious relationships I am not going to bother.
I will wine them, and dine them,
I rule them, fool them and be cool to them,
but settle down, no way, what do you take me for, a clown".

Unto him is born a child,
he is a father now, and his tone is now meek and mild.
However, this only last's for a short while,
soon he is out again running wild.

His child is older now, with an anger he wants to vent,
because for him, his dad has been always absent.
"Dad where were you when I got hurt at school?
Dad where were you when we ran low on gas fuel?
Where were you dad, when I needed you most?
dad now you want to know me, I am going to exorcise you from my life like
a ghost".

A few short years later that same man is quite as a mouse,
he is now bedraggled and will not leave his house.
His dreams and hopes have all been dashed,
his youth has gone in a flash.
He is permanently short of cash,
and everything he does is rash.
He feels he has committed the ultimate sin,
even his own child now disowns him.

When a man can see no further than his nose,
he very often knows not where he goes.
He is now such a sad destitute figure,
he has lost all his youth and charismatic vigour.

He now knows that a career raver,
has nothing in life to savour.

He wishes now for younger days,
he would do things now in different ways.
Everything he does now seems uncouth,
that's exactly what happens with a misspent youth.

Richard Todd

YOUNG LADIES PREROGATIVE

That young lady standing over there,
always wearing a smile, with time to spare.
Trying to look good and somewhat glamorous,
sometimes behaving impromptu and slightly amorous.

Another night out on the town.
Another night where her feet will not touch the ground.
Oh yes, she is a girl about town.

Young lady standing over there,
dress to kill, immaculate hair, without a care.
That man over there watching you; honestly he is not after your mind,
do you notice his eyes flickering, from the bottom of your legs to your behind.
You should let him know that your body is a temple or a shrine,
so he knows from the start not to get out of line.
Take it from a man who knows,
that's the way life is, and that's the way it goes.

Think of it this way, do you want a man that merely wants to play?
Do you want a man that only sees you in one way?
Do you want a man for just a day?
Or do you want a man that cherishes you in each and every way?
Its up to you young lady to set the standard you expect,
remembering always that it is your dignity and self esteem that you want to
protect.

Beauty has become a saleable commodity.
Real beauty lays in a certain level of dignity, integrity and modesty;
but quality on the other hand, is something you cannot buy,
no matter what you do and, how much you try.

What will you do young lady, when time has passed you by
and your body is no longer the apple of your eye?
That is the time that the quality in your character,
will come to the forefront and be the most important factor.
Remember this, physical beauty is a product of youth,
but quality is timeless and that's the truth.

Richard Todd

PHYSICAL CHASTISEMENT AS A FORM OF DISCIPLINE

Physical punishment of children is now frowned upon; it is seen to breach the principles of the Human Rights Act. Throughout the generations, we have been physically chastising our children, now we have been told by the Government we should not. The question that we have to ask ourselves is this, "Is the behaviour of our children now, better than it was 25 years ago, when we were allowed to physically punish our children? I would suggest that standards of behaviour have deteriorated considerably. It is my view one has to discipline one's own children and, that discipline will become an inner strength, when that child gets older. An inherent part of the disciplinary process is controlled punishment of a young child, particularly when the child is continually misbehaving. To quote a biblical saying, **_Proverbs 13:24:"He that spareth his rod hateth his son: but he that loveth him chasteneth him betimes._** Punishing a child is not the same as beating a child in an aggressive manner; rather it is a gentle; persuasive, form of correction. It is not the panacea to disciplinary problems, but it acts as a deterrent, it draws the line in the sand at a point in which the child should not cross. If the metaphoric line in the sand is not backed by firm action, the child will cross it with impunity. Are we now seeing the results of lack of affirmative discipline out on the streets and in schools up and down the country? Some would argue that physical punishment teaches the child violence and serves no purpose. My response to that is simply is to quote an old Jamaican saying, '**_a child that will not hear will feel_**'. Remember this truism, "Hard heads have to feel it to believe it".

Potential criminal behaviour starts at home. The corollary to that is that success also begins at home. I have seen mothers who dearly love their children so much so that they would never contemplate any physical affirmative discipline. They hold and caress there children almost as though the child was a pet, or a trophy. A few years later and that same mother is complaining; "I don't know what's wrong with that boy, he just won't listen". I have also seen mothers being shouted at and frantically kicked and punched by children no more than four years old, yet the mother laughs and smiles as though the child were being rewarded for good behaviour. In a year or so that child will be at school. The school will invariably have to deal with that child, where the parents have obviously failed.

PARENTAL RESPONSIBILITY

There is widespread concern from African-Caribbeans that state officials, such as schoolteachers and social workers have taken away their parental authority. This response, from a 27-year-old woman of African-Caribbean descent is typical:

"Society is destroying the Black family in the sense that the very same society who said to you, you cannot scold your children, you cannot speak too roughly to your child, will take your child away from you, put your child in a social environment. So the values that they passed down to your children are worse than what you would give, and it's the same society that would pick up your child that they took away from you in the first place, and put your child behind bars, and say he is a criminal. So can you see the vicious circle? So somehow we have to rewrite the agenda and say this is how we want to bring up our children, allow us to do that."

If we, as parents do not win the hearts and minds of our children at a young age, we will live to regret it. We should never lose sight of the fact that we are responsible for the behaviour of our children; if we fail in that fundamental parental responsibility, we don't only fail our children but we may also fail the generations to come.

TELEVISION AND FILM

Television and film nowadays are more about sex and violence than they are about education. Furthermore; the way Black people are portrayed on television remains negative. I rarely see anyone on TV that I can identify with. The Black characters in sitcom and drama are very nearly always negative and would not be a positive inspiration to any aspiring child. The Black community chastised the one Black sitcom "The Crouchers" aired on BBC1 at prime time. It was a comedy series based around a Black extended family. I have seen far more offensive programmes about which we, as a community have said very little. My take on the situation is this: "Is this not a good starting point?" The fact that "The Croucher" is on prime-time TV sends out a clear message; that mainstream television is beginning to think about our community. It is for us to take that forward build on this foundation, but not to knock it down. I remember the days when one saw a Black face on TV, wow, the whole family would gather around. If that Black face was in a movie, within ten minutes of the start of the movie; that person would be either killed, imprisoned or phased out, but he or she would not appear in the movie anymore.

NO MAN IS AN ISLAND

As a final thought on the family. 'No man is an island', no man can stand-alone. The family is the bedrock, not only of our very being, but also of our community and wider society. A family has unconditional love for each of its members and a share in a common belief that better must come. When I use the term 'family' I don't just mean the immediate, or nuclear family. I mean the wider extended family. In the eighties, the " Thatcher school of thought" was largely about prosperity for me, myself and I, it was considered to be 'enterprise culture'. It was a go get era, cut-throat and non-caring. It placed great strain on the family as stark choices had to be made. We are all charged with a responsibility to keep the family strong. I don't mean that we should live out of each other's pocket, quite the contrary I mean the family should act as a support mechanism in times of trouble or hardship. Remember, trouble comes in different guises and absolutely no one is immune. Me today, you tomorrow! Our parents and their siblings immigrated to various parts of the world USA, Canada, UK and the Caribbean which means we have cousins who are born American, Canadian West Indian etc. We should always remember to maintain ties, because it is a source of strength. When international boarders, or the ocean separates a family, but the family remain resolute, such a family is blessed.

CONVERT ANGER TO STRENGTH

Some young men on the street act as if the world is at their feet,
little do they know, to be hot on the street does not make them complete.
Some huff and puff and wear an indelible frown,
others walk around town, without knowing how to hold it down.

I know that a hungry man is an angry man,
and an angry man is a man without a plan.
Young man; life is too difficult to put into context,
if all you do is walk around upset and vexed.

Take the weight of hate off your shoulder,
don't wait until its too late or you get much older.
Time waits for no man, if you don't use it you lose it.
Remember this, a man that has wasted all his time, is a man in steep decline

Look to your family tree, to know where in life you should aim to be,
take strength from those solid folk around you.
Discard negativity and simple things that others do,
your father and/or mother may not be there for you,
it is up to you to look for others who can show you a way through.
Someone unconnected to you with focus and verve can easily be your mentor,
if those closest to you act as your tormentor.

Sometimes when your back is against the wall,
that's when the real man has to stand up tall.
Time now to remove the blindfold from your eyes,
time to see opportunity for what it is, without any skulduggery or disguise.

Richard Todd

CARE IN OUR COMMUNITY

INTRODUCTION

Several mental healthcare experts have agreed that Black people are over represented in psychiatric hospitals; their need for psychiatric help is revealed through crisis services and the Mental Health Act more often than for their White counterparts. Studies in London have shown that Mental Health Act admission rates are higher for African–Caribbeans than for comparable samples of White and other ethnic groups.

Black patients are the least likely to be recognised as having mental health disorders in primary care (White patients are the most likely) but, are the most likely to be referred to specialist services if mental disorder is detected. One suggested explanation is a lack of intervention, by community mental health services, early in the course of an illness. Other explanations from so-called experts, are that African–Caribbeans are actually more violent when they present with mental health problems, or that they are perceived to be so. Another explanation is failure to recognise signs of illness (by patient, family, GP or psychiatrist) until they are more severe.

MENTAL HEALTH

There is little doubt, from the available literature, that the incidence of schizophrenia amongst the African–Caribbean community is much higher in the UK when compared with Whites.

In 1993, The Mental Health Charity (MIND) published a policy on Black and minority ethnic mental health, which highlighted major concerns in relation to current mental health services, including that:

- racism impacts upon peoples' lives, on their mental health and on the services they receive;
- the diverse needs of people from different cultural, religious and ethnic communities, are often not met by the mental health services;

- Black people are more likely than White people to be picked up under section 136 of the Mental Health Act by the Police, compulsorily detained in hospital, diagnosed with schizophrenia and given high doses of medication.

Those in our community that have family members affected and afflicted by the condition know only too well the problems associated with the condition referred to as Schizophrenic Psychoses. I have seen this disorder, how it breaks the will of the family, how it tortures the mind of the sufferer, breaking them down before your very eyes. I've seen young men whom I knew in the past, sharp dressers, quick witted and proud; a few short years later, I see these same young men looking bedraggled, talking to themselves, in and out of the mental health care system. Back in those days, I did not know what had happened to them but now, with the benefit of hindsight and greater knowledge about mental health disorders, I have come to understand the pain and anguish they must have suffered. What a waste of young life and talent that now may never flourish. Parents can only sit idly by and watch their child, their future, their aspiration, disintegrate before their very eyes. Dare I say, it must be a living nightmare.

Very often, mental disorder begins in adolescence or early adulthood. Adolescence should be a carefree time on the way to adulthood, the gateway to life and all its wonders. In the case that I observed, the following symptoms were displayed; over a period of time the sufferer became withdrawn and agitated. This got progressively worse, disrupted sleep patterns followed, then the sufferer began to hear imaginary voices, and was tormented by the voices. Then came the irrational thoughts, like for example, the belief that someone wanted to kill the sufferer or focusing on an individual believing that individual to be the devil. At this point the sufferer entered a world of totally irrational fear and fantasy. If untreated this could become dangerous, as the sufferer honestly believes' these thoughts.

The thoughts of the sufferer are not always negative. Sometimes they may feel that they are in love with someone they have not even met, a movie star or singer for example. Sometimes these thoughts can manifest themselves in violence. The real difficulty for the family in the past was the general lack of interest exhibited by the healthcare system. General Practitioners were uninterested until the sufferer had a breakdown, and then they would suggest that the Police be called, particularly if violence or the likelihood of violence was involved. When the Police deal with a mentally disturbed patient, they arrive in full protective clothing including stab and bullet proof vest, they handcuff the sufferer and transport them to the local psychiatric hospital, where he of she is assessed and, if need be, Sectioned under the Mental Health Act. This allows the hospital to detain the patient for a specified period. It is only at this point, when things have reached an all-time low, does the healthcare system intervenes. If the family of the sufferer know the sufferer is about to have a breakdown and the family contacts the hospital, the hospital will only advise that the family contact the Police. This is what I call "The revolving door cycle," where the sufferer has a breakdown, calls the Police, the sufferer is taken to hospital, only to be released a few weeks later when yet another breakdown leads to a repetition of the cycle.

HEALTH CARE SERVICE RESPONSE

The healthcare system, in recent years, has improved in its practice of mental health care. The National Health Service, (NHS) have joined forces with Local Authorities to provide a one stop out reach service, where patients can attend a local clinic to seek assistance. There are now also psychiatric nurses to visit the patient at home who, in severe cases, can administer injections. The speed of diagnosis has also improved. Nonetheless, the community must be mindful of the fact that we are more predisposed to this illness more so than any other communities; and there is no underlying reason for this. Should we indeed be looking further a field for clues about mental disorder, is mental disorder amongst the black community widespread, in Africa, America or West Indies, do they suffer similar rates of mental care disorders? It is an area that warrants further investigation by the Health Professionals.

THE 'CARE IN THE COMMUNITY' EUPHEMISM

'Care in the community' is a euphemism for "care within the family." In my view; 'Care in the community' is an illusion, not a solution, it could even represent a danger in the community. The rights, wants and needs of the family are often ignored in favour of the rights of the sufferer who, very often, is not in a position to make valid decisions regarding his/her own condition. The truth of the matter is that care of the mentally impaired is held as being too expensive for individuals, who the Government believes are unlikely to contribute to the economy in any significant way. Therefore, there is a general reluctance to effectively fund this particular area of healthcare medicine. Remember this, the acid test of any civilised society is how well it looks after its sick and infirm.

We can clearly see, that mental-health care issues do not only disproportionately effect the UK black community the problem goes wider and deeper. It is a problem that affects wider society also, with the ever-increasing pressure on the individual. We need to improve our understanding of this condition as a community, so that we may be more tolerant and provide assistance to those affected, whilst addressing the underlying factors, which give rise to this debilitating condition.

We need to collectively demand of the Government, greater resources to research this problem. At the same time we must insist on greater transparency from the health service in terms of what it is doing to combat conditions which give rise to 'Care in the community'. In line with this, we need to see timetables and targets set by the Health Service, outlining where they see mental health disorder going over the next ten years, and what systems they expect to be in place by then to control or tackle it.

We also need to look at ourselves in terms of our lifestyle and the way we behave generally. Are our young men too aggressive; too macho, too hyperactive. Whatever the reason, we must objectively look inwardly if we are to find a way to manage this disorder. The taboo that most of us have regarding mental health is an impediment to objective thinking. To dismiss someone merely as "a mad man/woman or gone off their head" is shallow and foolhardy, because when illness comes calling, it is not a discriminator. ***Today that man over there , tomorrow a member of your family.***

A LOST MIND

A mind in turmoil.
A mind in freefall.
A mind tormented.
A mind lamented.

In a world where only the strong survive,
the bottom line objective is to stay alive.
You try to be good, as you know you should,
heaven knows you are simply misunderstood.

Some think you're bad.
Some think you're sad.
Some think you've been had.
Some think you're simply mad.

When a mind is confused,
and refuses to be infused.
Some think that such a mind is something to be feared,
not even contemplating that it might be slightly impaired.

Care in the community,
relies on a solid level of unity.
Don't snub that man struggling to control his mental health,
try and help him even if you do it by stealth.
As you know only too well without health there can be no wealth.

I feel his pain, oh what a shame,
I know he is not the one to blame.
All I want is for you the community to feel the same,
its your hearts and minds ,on this matter, that I want to claim.

Richard Todd

CHAPTER X

PLANNING & LEADERSHIP

INTRODUCTION

We have to start planning for our future as a community. In business we would refer to this as Strategic planning. Strategic planning is the longer-term analysis of where we want the community or enterprise, to go and how we intend to arrive there. In other words, it is the determination of long-term goals and objectives for the community/enterprise, the adoption of courses of action and the allocation of resources in order to achieve these goals. We have to begin to think like organisations. It is accepted that we are not one homogenous group, we are all different in our own way. Nonetheless, we must begin to think as an entity if we are to compete effectively, and have a positive role in society.

STRATEGIC PLANNING

Strategic planning is not just a business skill, it is also a life skill. After all, if we want to be successful, we must first plan. I don't know of anyone successful who has not planned and worked towards that success apart from those lucky enough to win the lottery or pools! Even successful sports personalities have to plan. Footballers for example, start to learn their craft from as young as five years old. David Beckham; one of the most successful footballers this Country has ever produced, trained with his dad as a young boy for hours on end, whilst other boys his age would be out playing. If we draw an analogy with our own life experience, planning probably started when we were at school. We all had visions and dreams of what we wanted from life. What we did not necessarily know at that time was the way to achieve our goals. What we did know, or at least our parents knew, was that if we were going to be successful, education would play a pivotal role.

How often have you got up in the morning to go to work and wished you had enough money not to have to work for a living, in order that work was superfluous, and therefore not compulsory. That is essentially a dream, it has no credence and in reality; a situation that can not be achieved in the short term. However, in the longer term it may well be achievable, hence planning. Clearly, planning in itself will not achieve your goals, but an honest belief in what you're doing, along with commitment and drive, is a move in the right direction. You can work hard all your life, at the end of which you have little or nothing to show for it. Its not for lack of hard work, rather, its how you work and for what goal. In a society where consumerism is king, it is easy to fall in the pattern of working merely to consume, this can become an end in itself.

A community without strategic planning is akin to a rudderless ship drifting in no particular direction, which in turn could undermine the success of the community, or indeed the success of the individual concerned. Furthermore, from a personal perspective, if you have no plan, you have effectively abandoned your future to fate. What a sobering thought! It is also worth noting that good planning is crucial to day-to-day decision making, it provides a framework in which decisions can be made.

THE PLANNING PROCESS

The process of strategic planning will, therefore, encompass the following;

- Setting community goals.
- Appraising the community resources.
- Analysing technological political and social trends.
- Assessing alternative paths.
- Producing detailed action plans and budgets.

The planning process is by no means hard and fast, but a good achievable plan will have the essential characteristics as outlined above.

The key to our future success is how well we adapt to the changing environment in which we now live. We should all now be planning to utilise the technology that is available to us as a means of improving efficiency and effectiveness.

"People often say that this or that person has not yet found himself. However, the self is not something one finds, it is something one creates." The bottom line in any planning process is the people, the human element if you like. It is imperative that we continually appraise ourselves objectively and consistently, with a view to empowering ourselves to enable us to achieve our goals. Listed below are the type of questions we should be asking:

- Do you know your strengths?
- Do you know your weaknesses?
- Do you know how to communicate effectively in a difficult situation?
- Do you know what non-verbal signals you are displaying?
- Do you know what you do that causes conflict?
- Do you know what motivates you?

Remember this, it is you the individual that is charged with the responsibility to develop yourself in a positive way; no one else can do it for you. Others may *help* you, *support* you, *push* you, but it is you that must *do* it for yourself.

LEADERSHIP

ESSENCE OF LEADERSHIP

There is a lack of leadership within our community. Without effective leadership we have no real direction and will only be able to move along issue to issue, crisis to crisis. If the Governments wants to engage the Black community, they don't know with whom or where to start. Very often we look to African-Americans for leadership rather than from within our own ranks. Others within our community have risen to prominence within institutions which may, to some degree, help our struggle, but this is no substitute for leadership. We cannot look at Black Members of Parliament as community leaders, they have a constituency to represent and they may have to tow the party line. Others may have risen to prominence thanks to their activist past, rather than being a strategist or leader.

What is leadership? You may well ask! For the answer we must look to management theory because leadership is an inherent part of the management process. Leadership is defined as; "The art or process of influencing people so that they can strive willingly and enthusiastically towards the achievement of group goals." There are various styles of leadership; autocratic, democratic or free-rein. The autocratic leader is defined as; "one who commands and expects compliance." The democratic style is, "one who consults subordinates on proposed actions or decisions." A free-rein leader is "one who gives subordinates a high degree of independence". Perhaps the best example of this is the Government, they lead the citizens, but they don't dictate.

CIVIL RIGHTS

"Agitator" was a term segregationists used to describe leaders of the Civil Rights Movement like Dr. Martin Luther King. Dr. King and others who talked the talk and walked the walk during the Civil Rights Movement (literally, from Selma to Montgomery for example) did far more than just shake things up. They demonstrated a brand of leadership that is not unfamiliar to African-Americans who take on positions of leadership. The leaders of that movement were on the front line of a different kind of battlefield, but one not without its dangers. Even those leaders who did not share Dr. King's notoriety did share the risk of paying the ultimate price, and many of them did. That is leadership in the black tradition.

Africana.com, an online magazine, first published the above summary June 2003.

Even though I was a child at the time, I remember the day Dr. Martin Luther King fell to his assassin's bullet. I was about 10 years old at the time, but I remember how sad it made my parents, I did not fully understand what was happening but what I did feel was a profound sense of loss which was overwhelming. How could someone thousands of miles away have such a philosophical effect upon us?

Here was a Black leader in the true sense of the word, whose sphere of influence went well beyond the boarders of the United States of America and touched others both Black and White. Not everybody agreed with Dr. Martin Luther King at the time, but he commanded respect and he had a vision of equality and diversity that would reach out to all who were affected or afflicted. History has taught us that when leadership and spirituality are compounded; there is a sense of fusion and purpose. Nowhere is this more evident than in the Dr Martin Luther King story.

In the same era there was another famous African-American leader Malcolm X. Yet again his leadership was based on spirituality (Muslim) linked with civil rights. His stance was quite different to Dr King's in that he did not believe in the concept of non-violent struggle. Even Malcolm's surname "X", was a powerful statement; "X" being the mathematical symbol for unknown. Malcolm believed that his original surname was given to him by the slave masters of previous generations and, therefore, he refused to use it.

Malcolm X, at the age of 39 was to pay the ultimate price for his leadership and beliefs; he was murdered at the hands of assassins. The legacy of Malcolm X lives on today, it is just as relevant now as it was then.

Black US Congressman, John Lewis, was only 15 when the influence of Dr. King was to woo him into joining the Civil Rights Movement. Congressman John Lewis stated that the aim of the Civil Rights Movement was not to overthrow or to takeover, but to redeem and reconcile with fellow man in an open and good society, by means of non-violent resistance. Therein lies the lesson for us as a community within the United Kingdom, we too want a society, which is just and fair, one that recognises diversity and embraces it.

For any leadership to be effective it must be supported by effective organisational arrangements. No leader can operate in a vacuum. It is said that good people can make any organisation work. Organisation is a word many of us use loosely, but I define organisation in the management sense as, "People working collectively within a group to achieve the aims and objectives of the entity to which they relate."

To be involved with issues of race or diversity, for some professionals within our community is seen as being *persona non grata,* an area they just can not or will not venture into . It will be frowned upon by the organisations which they rely on for earning a living. Others within our community do not have time to get involved, and for others, it's a simple case of inertia and apathy. As such, the people who could do most for the community are likely to remain sidelined for the foreseeable future. Consequently, we do not necessarily have the best brains fighting our corner as a community; this is a great shame. However, the African-American and South African experience has shown us that great strides can be made with effective leadership. Dr Martin Luther King, or more recently, Nelson Mandela, a legend in his time, personified this idea. I am not saying that any leader would have to be of that calibre, quite the contrary; what I am saying is that we have no effective leadership whatsoever and that we are desperately in need of some.

The 'Race' issue is controversial by its very nature. Any Black leader will invariably struggle with what is often a thankless task. Much of the inertia will not come from other communities but from within the Black community. Some of us will feel that we are not able to compromise ourselves for the better of our community as a whole. Others will grumble quietly at the direction taken by the leaders, whilst some will sit back and criticise to the point of disillusionment. There is absolutely nothing wrong with constructive criticism. In fact, good leadership needs the stimulus provided by constructive criticism. This is the best way to develop and grow in stature. However, when criticism is destructive, divisive or does not add value to the debate, it can undermine the aims and objectives of the leadership. Having said this leadership must be tapered with accountability and transparency. In other words: decisions taken must be clearly linked with the aims and objectives of the leadership.

THE ROLE OF THE CHURCH

INTRODUCTION

The role of the church has always been an enigma within the Black community. It's not at all clear whether the church wants to lead from the front, or to act as the conscience of the community. We, as a community, have never strayed very far from the church, even if some of us only go to church to hatch, match and dispatch, if you excuse the terminology. Yet the Black church is growing at an amazing rate, which tends to suggest that the community wants and needs some spiritual guidance, some theological direction and, dare I say, some leadership. Whether the church is in a position to provide this is not clear, but what is clear is that some of the churches are now gearing themselves up to meet the challenges of the community.

GOVERNANCE IN THE CHURCH

In order that the church can play a more practical role within the community, it needs to be resourced more effectively. Many churches have recognised this and have begun to undertake the provision of various community services, such as; nursery care, youth work and support for senior citizens. To this end, many churches have become charities, which effectively means they can operate without the impediment of taxation. But, to obtain and retain charitable status, churches do need to understand the principles of corporate governance, which in essence is transparency and accountability. Traditionally the church has limited experience of management or financial control. Faith organisations are characterised by their honest belief in delivering a service in their chosen area of expertise; but when it comes to governance and control, there can be little doubt that internal control takes a poor second place, if it exists at all.

For all voluntary organisations, or even small businesses in general, it is important to embrace the concept of Corporate Governance, the awarding of Government contracts and grant funding may well depend on it, amongst other things. I view Corporate Governance in practical terms, as a jigsaw puzzle where each piece, when fitted together, creates the whole picture. Outlined below are the following areas which must be included in the governance process:

1. Management body composition and structure.
2. Financial accounting and budget control arrangements.
3. Assets, insurance & security.
4. Banking arrangements.
5. Income control.
6. Personnel.

The African-Caribbean Evangelical Alliance (ACEA) held a seminar, in 2003, regarding governance, to which the Charities Commission and other agencies were invited. Joel Edwards, ACEA Director General, stated in his address to those attending, that the church needs to re-align its vision and be conscious of its responsibility and identity.

RUACH MINISTRIES

Ruach Ministries Christian Centre is one of the fastest growing Black churches in the United Kingdom. Its congregation is expanding week by week. Its appeal to people of all walks of life is clear and unequivocal, as it offers a message of hope and spiritual acquiescence. When I visited Ruach the church was full. The congregation packed the church to hear the pastor deliver a service of epic proportion. The energy and adlib spontaneity exhibited by the Pastor, is something that can only come naturally, it cannot be rehearsed.

There were 23 baptisms; some of the congregation spontaneously responding to the call from the Pastor to be born again, as to be born again is the only way one can be truly rid of the sins of the past. One man, whilst waiting for the Pastor to bless him, fell in a heap at the mere touch of the Pastor on his forehead. The atmosphere was spiritually charged and the congregation were very responsive to the call for them to praise the lord. What was clear to me was that the Pastor is an orator of great skill and that perhaps we the community, do need more orators who can both lead and direct. Having said this, the question I must ask from a community prospective, is this, "Can a great theological orator be a great strategist, or are the two, completely different subjects?"

PENTECOSTAL CITY MISSION CHURCH

The 'Pentecostal City Mission Church' has its roots firmly planted in Jamaica. Its founder member was closely associated with the Salvation Army. The church has grown over the years and, has become more international, with branches in the major cities in the United States of America, Canada and in United Kingdom. The 'Pentecostal City Mission Church' has a history of trying to help those within the community, who for one reason or another find they are lost in the austerity of life. They were one of the first churches in Jamaica, to open an orphanage for homeless children. The question I would ask is this, "How relevant is The 'Pentecostal City Mission Church' to members of the community who are disenfranchised, or others who have lost their direction?" Reverend McPherson of 'Pentecostal City Mission Church' pointed out; that the traditional church, has where possible, tried to remain close to the community. However, the Reverend points to funding as being the limiting factor, as most churches sought to target working people for church membership. This has to be contrasted with whom ancillary services are being provided for, which is primarily for people who perhaps have meagre resources (not working) of their own and therefore are unable to provide such services for themselves. The main aim of the church is to cater for the spiritual well being of the individual, but after that there is a 'cradle to grave' ethos that the church pursues, finance permitting. Nonetheless, this is not consistent across all branches of the 'Pentecostal City Mission Church'. The church provides services ranging from nursery care, youth groups, services for senior citizens and soup kitchens, along with other more traditional church services. Reverend McPherson explained; that the church was providing respite services, in areas long before Government set up the concept of social services as being Government responsibility. The church is ideally situated in a position where it can help with some of the problems facing the community, but to do this the traditional church has to re-invent itself with a clear vision alongside sound Corporate Governance. The 'Pentecostal City Mission Church' has gone some considerable way forward in readiness to face the challenge that is confronting the community as a whole.

Government agencies should recognise the fact that the Black church has a role, and therefore should include the church as part of the overall solution. The church can provide a sense of belonging and self worth, which Government Agencies would struggle to deliver. Particularly those churches that have a long track record, of delivering services to the needy within the community, along with sound Corporate Governance. We must recognise that the Government cannot throw money at possible solutions; also the Government will want 'value for money', quite rightly so. Therefore, the church must be ready and waiting to deliver.

What is clear, however, is that the Black church is one of the only institutions where we, as a community have come together of our own volition, in harmony. That in itself is a beauty to behold. As such it acts as a prototype of how we need to be engaging with each other in the wider community.

THERE IS A TIME FOR EVERYTHING

Everything in life has a season.
Everything in life has a reason.
Everything in life has its place and time.
Every time in life has its particular sign.

In the morning of your life there is a time to play,
always remembering that tomorrow is another day.
The morning of your life is also a time to learn,
in-order that later life you will have the capacity to earn.

For every plus in life there is a minus.
For every good, there is a bad.
For every strong one, there is one who is weak.
For every loud one, there is one who is meek.
For every asset there is a liability.
For everyone with strength and ability,
there is another who lacks a basic level of agility.
Yes my friend, it is difficult to make sense, of a world with so much
nonsense.

When you're young it's all about fun,
but too much fun leaves important things undone.
Everything has an impeccable balance,
and there is a balance to be had in the pursuance of your talents.

The evening of your life is a time for soul searching and reflection,
not everything you have done in life will be of absolute perfection.
We are all human and make mistakes along the way,
but tomorrow my friend, is yet another day.

As time leaves it's indelible mark on your body and mind,
you know instinctively that your younger days are now behind.
Where did the time go? I honestly just don't know.
All I know is I had a jolly good go.

When the day turns to night, everything is out of sight,
you now feel you have seen the light,
You fought with all you might.
You fought so many seemingly necessary and some unnecessary fights.
You even feel you've gone some way to having put the world to rights.

The darkness of the night is upon you,
all the events in your life appear before you,
there is nothing more you can do.
It is now time to get some heavenly sleep,
not a bleep not a peep just a quite deep sleep.

Richard Todd

CHAPTER XI

BUSINESS PHILOSOPHY

INTRODUCTION

W e cannot really engage with the modern world unless we have the education, knowledge, understanding and the where-withal to do so.

We, as a community, must think about the economic game we are in. We live in a capitalist world, which is the reality of where we are now, and we must accept that. That means we must begin, therefore, to understand some basic economic ground rules, such as:

- Purchasing power.
- Opportunity cost.
- The Art of saving.
- Investment.
- Banking .
- Understanding business.

If we fail to understand and grasp these basic concepts, we will be destined for a life of mediocrity.

PURCHASING POWER

Who is the real beneficiary in a simple purchase transaction, the consumer or the retailer? Who is making the profits and where are those profits going? Until one knows the answer to these questions, one is boxing in the dark. Economists refer to purchasing as voting with sterling, or the dollar bill. When one purchases a product; one is met-aphorically voting for it, by contributing to the organisation's profits. One is effectively saying to the supplier, "We like what you're doing, please continue, and we, the community, the consumer will support you and help you and your shareholders to even greater profits.

When we purchase goods and services from an entity or organisa-tion, we must ask ourselves some basic questions about the organisa-tion, such as; Would that organisation:

- employ you, or your child or any member of your family? or
- award any contracts to you or your family? or
- fund any local community activity.

If the answer to all these questions is '**no**', then you should consider taking your custom elsewhere. The spending power of the Black community in the UK runs into millions of pounds, but we never really ask for anything in return from those fat cats who are profiting from our consumerism; we spend without thinking about the wider implications.

OPPORTUNITY COST

When we buy expensive designer products, that's all well and good if we can truly afford it. I should point out that there is nothing wrong with consumerism; the fact is, we must, physiologically, consume to live, so in essence there cannot be anything wrong with buying good quality produce. The question I have is this; "Are designer goods always of superior quality to less well-known brand names?" When we look at a product and think about buying it, what is the opportunity cost? The economist defines opportunity costs as; "the opportunity foregone for the sake of the purchase in question." When one looks at the opportunity forgone objectively, we may consider the following: Could a similar product have been purchased at less cost but of the same quality, or could the money have been saved and invested? I call this type of evaluation process, "obtaining value for money." Unless we begin to embrace this concept as individuals and as a community, poverty will always be just around the corner.

THE ART OF SAVING

Those who save their money will be more likely to obtain business success as savings are a pre-requisite to investment, particularly for those of us of humble beginnings. The only way to progress towards business investment is to save. For example, if I earn £100.00 per week, I should set a target of what I expect to save on a weekly basis. Lets say I saved £20 per week, at the end of the year I would have saved £1040.00, not much you may say, but then I start earning interest, and I continue to save, in a few short years I have a considerable sum. I am now in a position to move from being a saver to investor. Financial institutions will now take me seriously as I have demonstrated a level of financial management. How often have we heard the saying "money does not grow on trees?" We have all heard that saying so often, but said in isolation it has negative connotations. What is not said, to counter this negativity, is that "money does grow through investment". This is how we need to think, as individuals and as a community. The success that other communities enjoy is based on this very simple yet effective premise.

INVESTMENT & BANKING

Investment is the seed from which longer-term profits or yields are made. Business success can only be achieved through investment. Investments can be defined as "the placing of one's assets at risk with the overarching aim of obtaining some financial or operational gain in the future." Assets can include;

- Money.
- Time.
- Stock.
- Property.
- Expertise.

Some entrepreneurs borrow funds in order to invest. Such entrepreneurs are considered risk takers. It follows, therefore, that any rewards such risk takers make are deserved. If we extend our thought process to the private sector industries, it would be fair to suggest that most, if not all, of these industries would have been created through investment and risk. The question we need to ask ourselves as individuals is this, "Are we risk takers, are we balanced risk takers or are we risk adverse". Real wealth, real independence, is the reward afforded to the successful risk taker, the corollary to this is those who take no risks can never really have true independence, also earnings are limited to pay structures. I am not suggesting for one minute that we should all jump up and become risk takers, what I am saying is that we need to be mindful of how investment works, particularly those of us who are parents. Children tend to pick up on the parent's habits and, if you are talking and thinking about investment your children will be more inclined to think about it themselves when their time comes.

We, as a community, should think very carefully about where we save our money. We should look at banks and building societies in a different light and start making them work for our business. We must remember that some financial institutions are more concerned about their shareholders than they are about us as customers. We should look more closely at banking policy, not only in terms of employment but also how they assist small businesses. We should be thinking about organisations that are objective in the manner they deal with customers and if in doubt, speak to conscious qualified financial advisors.

UNDERSTANDING BUSINESS

If we are to flourish as a business community, we need to understand and educate ourselves in the ethics, roles, responsibilities and procedures, of business. After all, we are living in a society where business is key. You cannot go anywhere now and not encounter some form of business, in one form or another. For example, you visit your General Practitioner, he or she is running a business, his/her business is delivering health care. You literally open your front gate and you are confronted with people going about their business, whether it be digging the road or teaching someone the Highway Code, it's all business. I have heard people say; "I don't understand business, I have not got a head for business". My answer to that is; "How can you not have a head for business, when every day you make economic decisions?" When you go shopping, decisions have to be made as to what to buy and whether or not you can afford it. This is essentially an economic decision, as you are seeking to utilise limited resources, i.e. cash. Every profession, any walk of life, irrespective of whether it be, science, medicine, law, accountancy or even the paper round child, its all business. "Business as usual," the cornerstone of any capitalist society. If you don't know the rules of the game, how can you even begin to play, let alone compete, in the game.

RED EYE CONCEPT

Historically, many of us who are successful professionals or entrepreneurs, do want to talk about it. The unspoken ethos is "don't discuss your business with strangers"; to avoid what is loosely referred to as the "Red-eye concept," (which means one begrudging the success of another, a Jamaican term). My response to such a view is this, "If I do not talk about my business, then whose business am I going to talk about, someone else's business"? If we, as a community adopt this concept, as a strategy, are we not in danger of becoming a community of gossips? Are we so afraid of the "Red-eye" concept, also aligned to "the crab in the barrel concept", (where one crab tries to climb out of the barrel the others pull him back), that we are prepared to abstain from any meaningful dialogue vis-à-vis business? Often, in the community, I hear people say, "That brother or sister has money".

Very often there is no further information about the individual other than simply they have got money. This type of thinking is counterproductive, unless we talk about what we do and how we do it, the next generation will be devoid of a rich source of information. As a result, we are restricted in the free flow of knowledge between ourselves and, as such we as a community will suffer from what I call 'information suffocation'. Other communities openly discuss their business, they write books, and run seminars; they give interviews, they write in magazines, they communicate. We, need to do the same, impart our knowledge to others so that they too may have the opportunity to thrive.

ROLE MODELS

The youngsters look towards sports personalities and singers, rap artists etc, as role models. They are not considering being professionals (doctors lawyers accountants etc), entrepreneurs or trade persons. There is nothing wrong with being a sports person, it's all good, but what are the realistic chances of achieving it. The essence of a real role model is being someone that can be emulated by others. The truth of the matter is that top sports personalities, singers and film stars can not easily be emulated, and they can only have a limited value to youngsters struggling in the 'real world'.

SPREAD OF WEALTH

When individuals achieve high sport or musical accolade within the community, it very often follows that such personalities make huge sums of money. I call this the "*few earn lots, but lots earn few*" syndrome. This is excellent for the individuals concerned, it may indeed give us light relief as we watch them perform on our televisions, but it does precious little for us as a community. For example if one individual makes £10 million, his marginal propensity to consume is limited to his/her wants and needs. They may want a bigger house or a faster car, but it will mean very little in what services they will want from the community. So, therefore, there is little spread of wealth within the community. By contrast, if you have 100 individuals earning £100,000 per annum, the marginal propensity to consume has increased one hundred fold. These individuals will want goods and services, some of which can be provided by the community; hence we have a better spread of wealth. Other communities benefit greatly from this better spread of wealth, in that they are better represented in the professional and business areas, hence they have a more economically viable community. However, the bottom line is this, we need more professionals and entrepreneurs or so-called risk takers, people with vision, focus, energy and drive. It is they that will create the real wealth within the community. Business excellence should be seen as a cornerstone of our future. We, as a community, should encourage entrepreneurial spirit wherever possible. <u>Entrepreneurship</u> and business is the key to self-determination and also a stronger community; indeed, a stronger society. It is, therefore incumbent on us as parents, wherever possible, to train and expose our children to the rigours of business, along with ethics and integrity. The earlier children begin to understand the rules of business, the earlier these children will develop a sense of independence and awareness, and they could grow to be business men and women, successful beyond our wildest dreams.

ITS ALL ABOUT BUSINESS

The capitalistic acid test is, undoubtedly, business success.
Have integrity, energy, focus and determination and the lord will do the
rest.
In order to effectively compete,
you must have no concept or notion of defeat.

Life today is about me, myself and I,
All the more reason for you and I to try.
Business is not for the faint hearted,
but you don't know how good you are until you have started.

From the day you're born you compete for limited resources,
until the day you die you are subjected to market forces.

You must plan to a man, and work to a plan.
If you cannot heed, you will not succeed.
If you cannot learn you will find it difficult to earn.

Remember this, failure is not falling down on attempting to pursue a
scheme.
Failure ,is not getting up to find another way to pursue your dream.

Richard Todd

CRAB IN THE BARREL

Sometimes you have to play the fool, before you can catch the wise.
You then have to catch the wise, before you begin to realise.
The 'red eye' impostor is amongst us, in heavy disguise.
Be weary of their deceitful lies.
It is not you, but your success they fear and often despise.

What possesses one to begrudge the success of another?
When they themselves don't even attempt to bother.
Success should be applauded and where possible imitated,
it should not be frowned upon or hated.
Remember this, haters can never be creators.

However my friend, the 'Crab in the barrel' syndrome,
forces many a man to go alone,
and seek his fortune and success on his own.
However, it's the community that suffer the consequences,
of this stupidity and incessant intolerances.

Please for the sake of the community, leave the man to achieve his plan.
Where ever possible give him a helping hand.
Learn from him if you can,
and only then will you begin to understand, that no man is an island.

You should take that negative energy,
and covert to a positive synergy.
Think about this, success favours those who contest,
not those who detest others, who are merely trying to do their best.

Richard Todd

CHAPTER XII

PROOSALS

INTRODUCTION

It would be remiss of me to point out issues and concerns within our community, without putting forward some proposals on how we might tackle some of the problems that beset us. My Internal Audit background, dictates, that where I uncover a problem a finding, that I endeavour to formulate some recommendations, by means of which, the said findings and concerns can be dealt with appropriately. One Chief Accountant once told me, rather tongue in cheek; "Richard, don't tell me or give me problems, give me solutions". Well I do not purport to have all the solutions, quite the contrary, but as a man who believes in systems and controls, I am keen that we set up the mechanisms and controls, along with a more robust mental attitude within our community, that will help to provide the solutions. We must empower various agencies and institutions to deal with issues and problems in a impartial and transparent manner. Please note, however, the proposals that I have documented in this book are not sacrosanct, nor are they the panacea to all our problems. However, the aim is to make us think more strategically and to engage the reader's mind about where we are as a community, and where we want to go, with particular regard to crime and education. We must begin to be proactive in the struggle for improvement; if we sit back and wait until things unfold, the solution will inevitably, become even more difficult. Some of the proposals you will see in this chapter, you will have already seen in earlier chapters. I have repeated them, in this chapter, for completeness and, in order that this chapter can be read as a stand-alone section of the book

Before I discuss my proposals; I should point out that I fully accept that the Youth Justice Board for England and Wales is in existence. The aim of the Youth Justice Board, is to prevent offending by children and young people. It delivers this by:

- Preventing crime and the fear of crime.
- Identifying and dealing with young offenders.
- Reducing re-offending.

My concern; with regard to the Youth Justice Board, as it stands, is that it appears, on face value, not to be delivering. It lacks a certain cutting edge. Furthermore, a quick evaluation of the Trustee Board Members showed that the Board is packed with academics. It is not clear whether any of the Board Members have a detailed understanding of youth culture, urban culture or popular culture. If one does not understand youth and urban culture, then I would suggest that it would have extreme difficulty in formulating an effective strategy to deal with youth crime. Some of the proposals documented herein could easily be linked with the Youth Justice System, but it might require change in the ethos of the Youth Justice Board for England and Wales.

CRIME

Tackling crime is not merely a Police responsibility; it is the collective responsibility of the entire community. Alas! I am not suggesting intervention where one sees a crime being committed, to do so could possibly endanger life. Rather, what I am suggesting is that the community has to be more willing to pass information law enforcement agencies, any other position is unsustainable, if we are to procure a just society. To facilitate this, it would be prudent for Government to explore the possibility of setting what I call an 'Independent Community-Based Agency', (ICBA). Having a community-based agency which witnesses, or people with evidence, could approach anonymously, would and in my opinion enhance the whole process of crime intelligence gathering within our community.

This ICBA would take information and pass it to the police. In so doing, the witness, or those with relevant information, is kept at arms length from the Police. This would indeed act as a buffer between the Police and a willing, if somewhat unsure community. I fully accept that the '**Crime-stopper**' initiative already exists, but what this approach would offer is a more community-friendly way of dealing with information, by people with an honest belief in what they're doing. This in itself will attract better information upon which the Police can act, and procure the evidence necessary for a conviction. I also accept that there is already an Independent Advisory Group set up by the Metropolitan Police, which is already conducting policy work. Notwithstanding this, I do see a role for a totally independent agency that reports to and is accountable to the community in which it serves. Furthermore, I have not discussed where funding is coming from for these proposals, as I am merely putting forward proposals which may fall on deaf ears, or may meet with disapproval:

The ICBA will also have a role in evaluating policy as it relates to the community. All new initiatives pertaining to serious crime will be assessed by the ICBA; in this way the initiatives are thoroughly vetted, not only the Government and the Police, but also by the ICBA, on behalf of the community. This would act to strengthen Police initiatives and give it credence and, therefore, support within the Black community.

- The ICBA will monitor the results of the Police, particularly with regard to serious crime within the community.
- The ICBA will annually report on all its activities. A copy of the report will go to the Home Office, Police and Greater London Authority. The report would be published and the main points should be reported in the ethnic and local media.
- The ICBA would prepare strategy documents vis-à-vis crime and liase with all Government and Local Government agencies as it sees fit, in order to discharge its responsibilities effectively. Any such strategies must be both crime-preventative and crime-detective in nature. Remember it is better to prevent crime than have to detect crime; Further the ICBA will market initiatives within all communities, the aim being to win the trust and confidence of not just the local communities, but wider society also.
- The ICBA will be involved in the production of a youth policy, to break the cycle of crime. To oversee pilot schemes, in conjunction with other institutions, with particular regard to school and after school behavioural problems as well as general, anti-social behaviour. Such schemes should not shy away from dealing vigorously with unruly anti-social children. The ICBA should feed into the work of the youth task force mentioned later in these proposals on education.
- The ICBA will comprise of professionals from different backgrounds, lawyers, ex police, accountants and teachers, church/faith representatives, and others that have an honest belief in the cause, particularly those who have been through the system and have first-hand life knowledge.
- The ICBA will act as the eyes, ears and conscience of the community. But it must seek to avoid elitism and to always be accessible.

We as a community, must demand more from our law-enforcement agencies, but we must also work with and support them in the war on crime. Crime is too huge an enemy for us not to be involved.

DRUGS

Parents must watch their children for evidence of substance abuse. It is best to talk to the child well before the child reaches an age where he or she can partake. There is no easy answer to the drugs menace; it is a problem facing society as a whole. What we do know, however, is that young children are at risk from suppliers which see them as a means of cultivating future market demand. In essence, the drug suppliers are doing what designer-goods marketing managers are doing, targeting children. Get children on board and one has a demand line for the future. It is every parent's primary duty to try to safeguard his, or her, children.

We should encourage whistle-blowing amongst our school children, perhaps a child help-line, where a child can phone if he, or she, believes a child they know is a user or dealer. Such information should be confidential nor relied upon in court by the authorities. I accept that such a strategy may need to be given far more thought but, if we can intervene at an early stage as adults, we may avoid a greater evil.

CRIMINAL JUSTICE SYSTEM (CJS)

We, as a community are entitled to impartiality within the CJS. A system that operates without prejudice in respect of, sex, race, colour or disability, in the dispense of law. One way to boost confidence is for the CJS to employ more Black staff in all areas within the system. The Home Office has begun to set targets for the employment of Black staff. We as a community, however, need to be assured that;

1. The targets are reasonable.
2. That there are systems in place to achieve the target.
3. That there is a proper mechanism in place to capture data relating to employment.
4. That there are periodic meetings between management and the community representatives, to discuss progress.

YOUTH CRIME AND ANTI-SOCIAL BEHAVIOUR

The proposals set out below, are intended to try to break the cycle of offending behaviour by targeting youth and attempting to intervene. These recommendations rely on the goodwill of the community to reach a consensus regarding the anti-social and criminal behaviour of some of our young people. In reaching a consensus, it is hoped that the community will give support to these proposals; remember, discipline is a pre-requisite to education, and our future, one day, will be in the hands of our children. It is incumbent upon us to empower a body, entity or organisation, to help to tackle behavioural problems on the front line, as it were:

- The Government should contemplate the setting up of a 'youth taskforce', hereafter referred to as taskforce. This body should have the power to enter schools and colleges etc, whilst working alongside the Police and Local Authorities. The taskforce must be charged with the responsibility of identifying crime hot spots, focusing their attention on children that truant, or are unruly, or who engage in street crime. Such a taskforce must be multi-disciplinary in that it can arrest, detain, question and caution, children. It must be able to work with parents, the school and Local Authorities, at all levels. It should be allowed to conduct surveillance, with regard to school crime, and to take the necessary action. Sting operations and camera evidence will be a key method of operations, particularly the hot spots. A child with criminal intent should never be allowed to think that there is no consequence for thuggery or street crime.
- A taskforce panel should be set up. All cases handled by the taskforce must be adjudicated. The adjudication panel should consist of no less than three members, and should be made up of professionals, community leaders, the church etc. The panel will have far-ranging powers, from mentoring to detention, and even American-style boot camps. The ethnicity of the panel should, as far as possible, be representative of the ethnicity of the people being adjudicated.
- Any adjudication must have an appeals procedure; any appeal must be lodged within a specified time. Whilst this does not relieve schools of their responsibility, to educate and discipline children, it will run alongside schools in that

it will assist with the more disruptive and unruly children, who are potentially, or who are already engaging in criminal activity.

- For any such taskforce to be effective, it must operate on a metropolitan level, as opposed to a Local Authority level. A metropolitan approach will help to ensure a consistent approach across the Capital and other cities.

- Children that would benefit from mentoring should be identified by the taskforce, in conjunction with other institutions. These children should be instructed to enter a mentoring programme.

- A hotline to the taskforce should be set up, where members of the public could then phone when they see children behaving in an anti social-manner. The taskforce may not necessarily respond to the specific incident, but may deploy resources in an area where there is a perceived need. The hotline would neither add to nor diminish Police responsibility; it is designed to compliment it.

- General loutishness and loitering, should not be tolerated. All parents should be asked to sign a good parenting contract. In that contract it would clearly state, that if their child were picked up for any reason by the taskforce and there was evidence that the child had behaved improperly, or with criminal intent, that they will work with the authorities to look for a solution.

- On the back of the above proposal, it may be worth linking the fixed fine mechanism which is already in existence, (where parents are fined for tolerating their child's truancy from school) with other behavioural standards expected and agreed in the good parenting contract. The finer detail would have to be worked out but the concept, I believe, could help to focus the minds of parents on the idea that if their child does wrong, they the parent could end up with the bill. In so doing, forcing the parent to take some responsibility. The Schools should undertake the administration of the contracts. Parents are already being made responsible for their children's attendance at school with the possibility of fines for truancy; this proposal is merely building on that philosophy.

- Where there is overwhelming evidence of continual offending behaviour, the task force should have the power to arrest children, in the appropriate manner. The child's parent or guardian should be summoned immediately.

In assessing the child, the taskforce can recommend the child receive further guidance in good citizenship, or mentoring, etc. The parents have to be made aware of their responsibilities in no uncertain terms. Children must learn to conduct themselves in an appropriate manner. If they cannot behave, they must face the consequences and those consequences have to be sufficiently harsh to deter them from further offending.

- Sometimes its not always prudent to tackle the child on the street. It may be better to obtain photographic/video evidence of that child's behaviour, then visit the child at home unannounced. Alternatively, go to the school or in extreme cases and apprehend the child, in a visible way, once the evidence is irrefutable. In such case the parent should be summoned immediately. If we don't get to grips with the unruly child today, we will have to deal with the serious offender tomorrow.
- The taskforce will have a programme of school visits, speaking to the children, letting them know the role and responsibilities of the taskforce, warning them against street robbery, shoplifting, theft, anti-social-behaviour, drugs and truancy.
- The taskforce will develop a knowledge base of problem areas and issues. Where they see a gap in for example, recreational facilities, they should report this, so that appropriate Government and Local Government agencies can take note.

If we are to deal with crime effectively, we must tackle it at all levels. What begins as school truancy and bad behaviour can end in gun crime once the child has graduated.

MENTORING

It is incumbent on us as a community, particularly the men, to try and reach youngsters by mentoring them, talking to them, showing them a better way. We must give them a sense of hope and a sense that better can be achieved. We need to explain to them the importance of education. We have only to look at the experience of slavery to know that when education is denied, poverty is the result. Why, therefore, should the youth deny themselves the education that so many of our ancestors died for? Education is not just about money and wealth; it is about a sense of well-being, a sense of understanding the world in which we all live.

ROLE MODELS

Role models should be ordinary people, professionals, entrepreneurs, tradesmen/women, managers, not just sports personalities or musicians. After all, how many individuals can make money from art or sport, very few can score 25 goals in the premiership, or knock out Iron Mike Tyson. However, many of us can earn a reasonable living by just simply being good at whatever we choose to do. Good professionals can earn £75,000 per year, upwards. We, as a community, want more professionals and more entrepreneurs in order that we become a more balanced community.

PARENTS SUPPORTING SCHOOLS

Parents should seek to help their children in the following ways with regard to education:

- Develop understanding skills to help the child.
- Adjustment in lifestyle, regular sleep, etc.
- Reduction of negative influences, no video, DVD, or television in the bedroom.
- Monitoring phone calls.
- Monitoring use of the internet.

EMPLOYMENT CONSOLIDATION

When we hold any position within an organisation or institution, we have to treat it with due reverence, as we know that it is precious to us. If it is lost, we could be a long time unemployed, no matter what qualifications we have. I refer to this as the "consolidation strategy"; a strategy that dictates that one holds on dearly to what one has, building upon it in a structured way.

PAYING TO MUCH

Discard the pursuance of designer merchandise, unless you can associate such produce with quality. Remember, to pursue brand named products only because they are branded shows shallow thinking, its for the weak minded and those who have no vision. One always pays twice for such products, i.e. the amount of excess which one pays over and above the real value of the product and the opportunity lost, in respect of savings and investment. Save wherever possible, as saving are your investment for the future.

MENTAL HEALTH

As a community, we need to look inwardly, in terms of our lifestyle, and the way we behave generally. Are our young men too aggressive, too macho, or too hyper active, or is there a drugs problem? Whatever the reason, we must look inwardly and objectively if we are to find a way to tackle the mental health affliction and disorder that is affecting so many of our young people. The taboo that most of us have with mental health is an impediment to objective thinking. To dismiss someone merely as "a mad man/woman or gone off their head" is shallow and foolhardy, because when illness comes it has no bounds. Today that man, tomorrow a member of your family.

GOAL ORIENTED PHILOSOPHY

We have to be more goal-orientated. By this I mean that we must think more in terms of what our goals are and how we aim to achieve them. To this end, we need to be more involved in the policy development end of the strategic process and in the setting of targets and goals. Merely to sit back and challenge Government policy on education, or the Police when they set up a new initiative on crime, is a reactive approach. We must be at the forefront of policies that affect our community. Also, we have to move to a more strategic level of thinking. In five years time, where do we want to be? We must think "outside the box," so to speak, in an objective yet transparent way. We need to get the right people into the right positions, not necessarily those who are vociferous, but perhaps those who are focused and proud. This is the challenge that faces us in this decade.

GENERAL

The above proposals do not take into account what is already in existence. I know that there are various groups and organisations that cover some of what has been proposed in this book. Notwithstanding this, I have taken a clean sheet approach or what accountants' call "zero based budgeting," which is to build up from nothing. The idea being to create a blueprint of structures that can deliver not only the level of strategic thinking necessary, but also the operational know how. Remember, these are merely skeleton proposals, for you the reader to think about and, perhaps for Government Agencies to take note. However, it is you the reader, which must add body to these skeleton proposals, in order to give them life. Our long-term future depends on it.

WE ALL HAVE A ROLE TO PLAY

Society demands that you have a role,
and I know you don't like living off the dole.
"What have you done to better yourself, come on, you must do something,
or do you believe in quick money and the bling bling thing?"

What is money? It is a medium of exchange,
we need it to buy goods and services, and even get some change.
Without money there can be no economic freedom,
this is how the system operates in the United Kingdom.

Some say money is the root of all evil,
others say the love of money works hand in hand with the devil.
Our physiological needs dictates that we must consume to live.
We need money to help each other and sometimes to give.
The purchase of food and shelter, is key,
in our quest to climb the economic tree.

We need someone to mow the lawn.
We need someone to grow the corn.
We need someone to look after the sick.
We need someone to lay the bricks.
We need someone to provide transport.
We need someone in import and export.
We need someone to represent us in a court of law.
We need someone to uphold the rule of law.
We need someone to fly the plane.
We need someone to repair the drain.
We need someone to teach,
and even someone to preach.
This is not all we need,
but it is a start if we are to succeed.

The capitalistic free market has a strategic plan,
Adam Smith a famous economist called it, 'the invisible hand',
therefore we must all work towards our goals man to a man.
Everyone has a role to play,
and everyone must do it in their own particular way.

If you are not part of the economic system,
perhaps you should think objectively about what you do, or even list them.
Make no mistake someone living on a free rein,

is nothing other than an economic drain.
Over time society and the community can not afford you,
it is for you to find something constructive to do.
There can be no free meal ticket at this dinning table,
not if you are fit and physically able.
Remember this, every economy has its balance,
it is for you to find and exploit your hidden talents.

Richard Todd

CHAPTER XIII

CONCLUSION & VISION

THE IMPLICATIONS OF SLAVERY

There are so many issues that affect and afflict our community, with this in mind I have only attempted to discuss a few areas. There are other areas that are not covered to any extent within the body of this book, such as: employment, housing and the vexed question of asylum. It is not that I do not consider these areas as being serious because they are. Rather the contrary is true, I believe them to be so important that they have to be dealt with in a comprehensive and thorough way, perhaps in a future addition of this book, or another book.

The legacy of slavery is still very much a part of our psyche. We are a by-product of slavery. We were on the wrong end of a primitive capitalism, which needed cheap labour to power its industry. Cheap labour means cost of production is reduced. We know that profit is a function of turnover less cost. Therefore, cheap labour costs equate to greater profits. How would such a crude system fare with human rights today? Perhaps this was one of the greatest crimes against humanity within the last 250 years. In any war or conflict the victor gets the spoils and gets to write the history, that is why our history goes largely untold. In accounting terms, slaves were merely assets, perhaps to be recorded in the master books of accounts as "human chattel". The worth of a slave would have been measured in units of production. Where a primitive capitalism is fused with unadulterated racism and sheer inhumanity, one has the essential ingredient for slavery to thrive.

We should not, however, let slavery colour our decision making or judgement. Our shackles of the past can act as our reins for the future. We know there is no gain without pain. Wilberforce and others emancipated us from physical slavery. We did not emancipate ourselves. Nonetheless, it is only us that can emancipate our minds. In the words of the great Robert Nester Marley; *"emancipate yourself from mental slavery – who but ourselves can free our minds"*. We must never forget the past, but we must also embrace the future, with love and understanding for our fellow man. To harbour hate and ignorance will only serve to destroy those who hold such negative feelings. We must take heart from the fact that "yes" we survived as a people, and that we are here to grace our forefathers who lived and died in what must have been '**hell on earth**'. It is because they endured the pain and suffering that we are here today.

CURRENT AFFAIRS

Hitherto, there has been lack of cohesive, co-ordinated, strategy between all the various government institutions to deal with crime within the Black community. Operation Trident attempts to deal with gun crime in London but, to some extent; this is locking the door after the horse has bolted and therefore is a piecemeal approach. Other agencies, such as Local Authorities and schools work on an individual basis. School policies are determined by school Governors and, in some cases Local Authority Councillors. It is therefore, difficult for hard-pressed schools to have co-ordinated strategies with other Government agencies. In some areas the Police work with Local Authorities in a consultative manner. Above all, we must have some concern in regard to the behaviour of some within our community. There will come a point where we have to accept that some individuals within our community are lost. We must try to help them with the arm of hope and guidance. There are, unfortunately; others who may be beyond reach, the so called 'hard heads', Those who can't hear must feel the rod of correction, as some need to feel it to believe it. The question I put to you is this, "Are we, as a community, ready for that?"

Many of us have had negative experiences of the Police the "stop and search"(SUS) laws of the seventies. Changes were made to the SUS laws as a result. The McPherson Report, indeed; subsequently showed the Metropolitan Police to be institutionally racist, as a result of the Lawrence Enquiry. The Metropolitan Police themselves will admit that they have some work to do in terms of improving their standing and perception, within the black community. We must never forget where we have come from; because without knowing where we came from, how can we know where we are going? Nonetheless, we have to recognise that we do need the Police and that we have to change our entrenched attitudes towards working with the Police. Likewise, the Police have to change their attitudes towards us, which, we must accept they are trying hard to do. We are not all one, homogenous, whole; there are many different shades of black, we are a diverse community with many differences, good, bad and indifferent. Good policing will seek answers deeper than the colour of someone's skin. If one is blinded by the colour of another's skin, they will be unable to assess the content of that person's character.

The Police have a difficult job to do and we must recognise this. Criminality is the scourge of modern-day society and we "good Citizens" must help towards its elimination. Just think for a minute, if the police were not there, could we as a community Police ourselves? The answer has to be, a resounding, "NO!" We are simply not equipped for that. It follows, therefore, that we need to lend our support to the law-enforcement agencies. However, this support should not come without checks and balances to ensure accountability and transparency within the Criminal Justice System.

The real and decisive battle, is the war on drugs. Drugs in the community will bring elements of the community to its knees. Drugs do not only destroy individuals, they destroys the families associated with those individuals. Drugs being sold on the street to individuals are a direct attempt to kill those individuals, by slow poisoning. If we as a community are to progress, we must face up to our responsibilities with zeal. Our children have to be taught how to be good citizens and to fear illegal drugs; we cannot and should not, leave this task to the Government institutions. The drugs menace is singularly the biggest risk to our community today.

As a community, we must question whether or not we are facing up to our responsibilities, individually and collectively, with regard to our youngsters. We, as a community, have bought into consumerism in a very big way. We are not content unless we are buying designer-named products. Is it any wonder, therefore, that our children have taken it a step further, in that they now embrace the 'get rich quick' mentality, (the so called bling bling culture). The realism surrounding the get rich quick mentality is that in the longer term, it fosters real poverty on a personal level and in the wider community. I can comprehend someone paying more for a product because it's of better quality and, in principle there is nothing wrong with that. However, where I do have grave concerns, is when someone buys a product purely because of the brand (designer) name, paying above the odds, without reference to quality. As a community, this is an unnecessary outflow of funds to corporate organisations already awash with wealth. Furthermore, very little of such expenditure will ever be returned to our community.

In the longer term, education is the key. True wealth in a community comes through knowledge, skills and disciplines. One philosopher once said that education was a simple case of knowing "who is doing, what, to whom". Where one has education, one has the means to escape the shackles of poverty, which is ravishing our community.

However, discipline is a prerequisite to education; without effective discipline, the foundation for education is impaired.

The Black family is without doubt showing signs of decline; whilst this is also true of the wider society, this is particularly acute within our community. A strong family produces strong individuals who take comfort in the knowledge that they have a sense of belonging, which affords them unconditional support in times of hardship, whilst at the same time being a kindred spirit in good times. The sum of the individual parts is less than the family as a whole. In other words, together the family is stronger than if everyone acted as individuals.

Fathers have to be more responsible. It is a man's prime responsibility to provide for himself and his family. It is the extent to which this is achieved that will be the true judgement of that man, not his physical presence or his testosterone levels. A man that walks away from his responsibility is a man walking away from his future, towards the abyss. Can a man be so shallow as to think only about his own personal gratification, as opposed to that of his offspring or of the generations to come.

We as parents must acknowledge our responsibilities towards our children. Who teaches a parent how to be a good parent, or is it an instinctive process? We cannot allow our children to continue this downward behavioural spiral, we must intervene. This reminds me of an old; anecdotal, story my parents used to tell me. When they were children, any adult in the 'district' could and very often would chastise them and, if need be spank them. They would not dare tell their parents. It was a form of collective responsibly to discipline, and it worked. In those days there was a stronger sense of community, which appears to have been lost today, particularly in the big cities. Whilst I am not advocating this behaviour, what I am saying is "Have we really progressed or have we gone backwards? Are we so afraid of our children now, that we have abdicated our responsibility?" Is it the child that is now calling the tune and the adults are merely dancing to the music as orchestrated by the child? **"We need to get a grip and get a grip fast, or we will sit back and watch our aspiration for the future disintegrate before our very eyes."**

We have come a long way and we have a long way to go. Opportunity favours those with the vision to see it. Let us grasp the moment, seize the opportunity. We want, and need, to play a positive role in the betterment of society as a whole, based upon the principles of fairness, equity, and justice to all members, not only of our community but society as a whole. It was Dr. Martin Luther King, the African-American Civil Rights Leader, who said; *"I don't know what the future holds but I know who holds the future"*. I Have also heard it said, *"if you want to go fast go alone, but if you want to go far, go together"*. Lets go forward together and we shall go far.

MOTIVATIONAL MESSAGE

A good friend of mine sent me a motivational message, but when I read it I found that it represented our struggle so I would like to close this chapter on an inspirational note and share the message with you:

One day a farmer's donkey fell down into a well. The animal cried pite-ously for hours as the farmer tried to figure out what to do. Finally he decided the animal was old and the well needed to be covered anyway; it just wasn't worth it to retrieve the donkey. He invited all his neighbours to come over and help him. They all grabbed a shovel and began to shovel dirt into the well.

At first, the donkey realized what was happening and cried horribly.

Then, to everyone's amazement, he quietened down. A few shovel loads later, the farmer finally looked down the well and was astonished at what he saw. With every shovel of dirt that hit his back, the donkey was doing some-thing amazing. He would shake it off and take a step up. As the farmer's neighbours continued to shovel dirt on top of the animal, he would shake it off and take another step up. Pretty soon, everyone was amazed as the donkey stepped up over the edge of the well and trotted off!

Life is going to shovel dirt on you, all kinds of dirt. The trick to

getting out of the well is to shake it off and take a step up. Each of our troubles is a stepping-stone. We can get out of the deepest wells just by not stopping, never giving up! Shake it off and take a step up!

These are five simple rules to be happy:

1. Free your heart from hatred.
2. Free your mind from worries.
3. Live simply.
4. Give more.
5. Expect less.

BLESSED!

NIGHT THOUGHTS

The hour is coming, the day eases out of sight.
Soon you're surrounded by the majestic darkness of the night.
Sometimes in the stillness of the night your thoughts run wild.
Sometimes you even recollect situations that happened when you were a child.

In the midst of the night I recollect my mother saying "boy hold your head high,
and walk tall and look the world right in the eye".
However, now I am a man, I can now understand why.
In an oppressive world you either stand tall or hide in the corner living a lie.

The stillness of the night acts as a kind of escapism,
away from the rigours of toil, hatred, and even racism,
away from this wicked world in which we inhabit.
It is this time I choose to purge my mind of all negativity, as a matter of habit.

When your thoughts slowly melt into dreams,
you think of lavish themes with fanciful schemes.
I then suddenly remember, dreams are for those who sleep,
and tomorrow, what I sew, so shall I reap.
I then have an immediate urge to leap out my sleep,
as I think about my people running around like a long lost sheep.

Tomorrow, I pray that I shall awake from my slumber,
I know by daybreak, my lavish dreams will be asunder.
However, the strength of my will and ambition roars within me like thunder,
Is it any wonder I think like this, given the pressure I am under.

Oh what a night when the pendulum swings,
and each precious swing, signifies the passing of someone or something.
The quietness of the night has a way of exaggerating everything.
On a bad night I yearn for the morning,
on a good night I find it all so enthralling.
However, sometimes would you believe I here my calling,
I know then that I must stop stalling,
tomorrow I must awake early in the morning, and answer my calling.

Richard Todd

INERTIA CAN NEVER BE A SOLUTION

I don't claim to know all the answers,
I don't even claim to know all the issues.
However, I am a simple man,
with an uncompromisingly simple plan.

In putting together this book,
I hope you, the reader, will take time to look.
I have come to the unmistakeable conclusion,
that inertia can never be our solution.
This is indeed my contribution,
I know and you know it's not a resolution,
nonetheless, it's designed to eradicate a superficial level of confusion.

We, as a struggling and suffering community,
must come together in the majesty of humility.
We must continue to take the moral road,
as, only we know, on our backs we carry a heavy load.

On we must go on with the metaphorical fight,
as only we can influence our destiny, as we can now see the light.
We must take time to teach our children ethics, love and good behaviour.
As this world is so strange, that one day they may become our saviour.
In our quest for a better more equitable society,
we must teach the children integrity and propriety.

It was Martin Luther King Jnr who said "I don't know what the future
holds,
but I do know who holds the future.
Nonetheless, encapsulated in this book is the story I have to tell,
are we, the Black British community, beleaguered, bewildered or a bombshell?

Richard Todd

CHAPTER XIV

CHALLENGES

INTRODUCTION

Sometimes we have to challenge ourselves, ask ourselves searching questions, not so much about others, but about ourselves. We cannot sit back and expect others to safeguard our interest. We have to begin the process, by evaluating ourselves objectively. This chapter merely focuses on the specific challenges mentioned earlier in the book. It is designed in such a way that you the reader can now browse through each question systematically, as a means of challenging your thought process.

I can only ask you to come and sit at the dining table, it is you who must decide to eat. All I can do is make sure that the food is appetising and healthy. I do not claim to have all the answers, you may have some and others may have some, but together we must begin, collectively, to address some of the challenges.

CHALLENGING QUESTIONS

1. "Does our current problems surrounding education and dysfunctional families have their roots firmly planted in the days of the slave trade?
2. Carnival, partying and now, in an indirect way, raving, derives from rejoicing after emancipation. Are we now still in aftershock and is this the reason why we see raving or partying as such a high part of our social agenda?
3. We were taken forcibly from our homeland to shores far away, led like lambs to slaughter, yet we opened not our mouths. We lost our religion, self esteem, culture and our ability to determine our own destiny, yet we survived. Where, therefore, was our Truth and Reconciliation Commission?
4. Does the interbreeding of slaves in terms of the fittest of the fittest and the strongest of the strongest, create a physical thoroughbred, and could this be a reason why descendants of slaves excel so much at sport, where speed and power are of the essence?

5. Wilberforce's success at abolishing the slave trade does however, beg the question as to where the church was whilst the slave trade prospered for hundreds of years?

6. Have we exchanged one form of slavery for another? Did we really ever receive our 'free paper'? Or are we still running around like long lost sheep, whose lost their master and has gone astray?

7. Without knowledge of our past, how can we set out our road map, as it were, for the future? If we do not know where we are coming from, how do we know where we are going to? If we don't know who we are, then how do we know who we want to be?

8. If the West Indies is so pleasant why would my parents and many like them have wanted to leave such undeniable splendour, what was the driving force behind what would have been a drastic decision?

9. Since the fifties and sixties we have seen the living standards in the United Kingdom improve considerably, but this has not been echoed in the Third World. I can, therefore, understand and see why Jamaicans now, would want to leave Jamaica in search of a better life; the question is, "In what way is that better life procured?"

10. What have we, the Black community achieved, with our relative advantage over those wishing to come to the United Kingdom in pursuit of a better life, and should we be doing better?

11. Does Great Britain owe Jamaica a duty of care as its previous colonial master and before that, slave master, along with the sheer brutality of the slave trade?

12. Does independence mean Jamaica, and other countries like her, must go alone and pitch herself at the mercy of the world market?

13. Can the Motherland learn lessons, with regard to education and discipline of children, from its ex- colonies?

14. I urge you to think about this. Our parents and grand parents uprooted themselves from their loved ones and communities within the West Indies to travel to the United Kingdom. Is it not, therefore, incumbent upon us to move forward in a manner that will grace the opportunity the first generation have afforded us?

15. Are our children now beginning to frighten us, are they in the driving seat? If these children hold our future in their hands then what future have we got?

16. Can we put the problems we face as a community with regard to education solely at the Government door, or are we complicit after the act?

17. Could globalisation and the expansion of the European Common Market fuel the ever growing underclass in the United Kingdom?

18. If our community has no clear approach on how to deal with crime and anti-social behaviour, why then should we feel hurt if other institutions and communities impose a solution upon us?

19. I have heard Black community leaders say "the Black man does not manufacture guns" and at the same time ask where are these guns coming from. Surely its not the source of guns that's the primary issue, rather is it not, who has their finger on the trigger and what is in their heart?

20. The futility of gun crime is, in itself, abhorrent. Who gives one person the right to take the life of another? Has life itself become so cheap within our community? Where then is this animosity to each other coming from, what type of hatred or wickedness prompts a man to gun-down another?

21. The Government has introduced tough new sentences for those caught with firearms. But, in order for this to work, the Police will invariably have to stop and search. The question is, "Are we still not prepared as a community to tolerate 'stop and search', given our past experiences?" Or do we now forget the pain of the infamous SUS laws of the past, in order to safeguard our physical security in the future, given the level of black on black crime?

22. To my humble mind, is not gun crime on our street the real war, is this not the real front line and, is this not the real terrorism? Where, therefore, are our coalition forces?

23. The countless times I have visited peoples homes, and their little infant child is running around after 10pm at night. Is this the beginning of indiscipline, could this be tomorrows lout?

24. As a child I remember my parents saying to me, "you're a child and as a child you must maintain a child's place". Imagine telling a child that today, indeed what is a child's place?

25. The question that we have to ask ourselves is this, "is the behaviour of our children now better than it was twenty five years ago when, of, course we could physically punish our children?

26. What are we really doing when we engage in simple every day purchase transaction? Who is the real benefactor of a simple purchase transaction, the consumer or the supplier, and who is making the profits and where are those profits going?
27. The unspoken ethos is "don't discuss your business with strangers"; to avoid what is loosely referred to as the 'red-eye' concept, which means one begrudging the success of another. My response to that is "If I just talk about my business whose business am I going to talk about"?
28. Are we, the Black British Community, Beleaguered, bewildered or a bombshell?
29. Now that you have read the book, what do you think of it, did you find it informative and helpful, or boring and shallow?
30. If I were to write another book what issues would you like to see covered?

Please email your response to either blackshare.com or the author's email address bbeas_64@hotmail.com

In the words of a great Jamaican singer, Johnny Nash, *"There are more questions than answers, and the more I find out the less I know"*.

SIMPLE THINGS

Oh what a fool am I,
living a life that is a consummate lie.
Not stopping to ask the reason why,
just aiming high trying to reach the sky.

I am not at all clear what I want from this life.
Materialism and consumerism does not ease my strife.
Sometimes I think about my children and my wife,
But even then I still ponder on the meaning of life

Our time on this earth is so incredibly short,
we are merely passing through, like a ship in and out of a port.
One minute we are like a budding flower,
the next minute its all gone like a passing shower.

Perhaps life is not for us to reason why,
Ultimately, we hope we end up in God's great heaven in the sky.
Perhaps it is the simple things in life we should protect,
rather than going through life with regret and neglect.

Every morning I wake and when I see another day,
I give thanks just for that, come what may.
I just look around me at the trees, the flowers blooming and the children at play.
In that I see a beauty to behold, and I know the lord made it this way.

Sometimes in life it is not until you face the abyss,
that you can see the beauty in this world that exists.
We complicate things and then try so hard to understand,
why not just leave it in Gods capable hand?

Richard Todd

ONLY LOVE CAN CONQUER HATE

Love each other dearly,
and deal with each other fairly and squarely.
Haters can never be creators.
Only Love can conquer hate.
In this there can be no debate.

Love your neighbour.
Take time to savour.
Don't even bother to waiver.
To do this is entirely in your favour.

Be good, as you know you should.
Be bold sometimes, but never be cold.
Sometimes we have to be cruel to be kind.
We must always remember to leave foolhardy thinking behind.
Lets cut to the chase, no time to waste,
now we have the taste, we must pursue it in haste.

Being British and being Black,
its time to be focused and remain on track.
A view aired, Is a view shared.
This view I share is for those of you who care.
This is my Black British experience aired and shared.

Richard Todd

INDEX

A

B

C

D

E

F

G

H

I

J

K

L

M

N

O

P

R

S

T

U

V

W

Y

Z

ISBN 141202958-9

9 781412 029582